Rev. Peter Dinh Ngoc Que, CSsR
(The English Version by Tran Van Dien)

Memoirs of a Priest
Imprisoned
In
The Communist Reeducation Camp
(1975 – 1988)

Feb 23 , 03

Celebrating the Great Jubilee 2000

"If allowed to boast, I only dare to boast that God has blessed me with a great honor of carrying His Cross with Him"

IN REMEMBRANCE OF MY PARENTS

MR. ĐINH VĂN PHÁC
    He loved his son so much that he did not mind his old age when going to Camp Thanh Cẩm to visit me.

MRS. PHẠM THỊ HOA
    It is thanks to her intercession and daily prayers that I was called to be a priest.
    May God grant them His Grace in abundance, so that they could soon enjoy His Holy presence in Heaven.

GRATEFULLY TO:
    Soldiers, government workers and politicians in acknowledgment of their self-sacrifice in one way or another for the just cause of the nation.

SPECIAL THANKS TO:
    Phan Lan Anh Family for their sponsorship of this edition.

Rev. Đinh Ngọc Quế, CSsR
USA, March 30, 1998

INTRODUCTION

"A Catholic Priest In The Communist Prison" is Father Dinh Ngoc Que's memoir that describes in details his daily life during his 13 years in reeducation camps (1975-1988), and his following years after having been released from camps and also after his resettlement in the United States of America.

The memoir has unearthed some policies of the Communist party of Vietnam (CPV) toward the lives of the Vietnamese people and how Religious Faith helps prisoners survive the ordeals.

I. REPRESSIVE MEASURES AGAINST RELIGION.

Stories are told about the policy of religious persecution by the CPV:

- Religious practice in the reeducation camps is prohibited. Priests have to devise a plan to conduct "clandestine" Masses: secret arrangements for a

Mass at such a place as by the side of a well, in a corner of a sweet potato field, behind a bathroom or at an other hidden place. Sometimes, priests pretend to converse privately to help a Christian get peace in his mind or provide religious education to a new convert. Such a session is held between two persons. If more than two are involved, they walk side by side in an open area to avoid suspicion.

- Church properties have been confiscated: As a principle, all church properties such as schools, social services facilities, lands, houses for priests etc. have been seized by the Communist authorities and turned into offices or storages of the CPV. For example, the chapel at the Blood Spring camp in Bien Hoa has been used as storage; the one located at the Armed Forces of the Republic of Vietnam (ARVN) Signal Corps in Saigon has become a shop for vehicle repairs. All properties owned by the Redemptorist Congregation in Hanoi including seminaries and buildings to house priests bear the same fate; all of its land has been confiscated and housing projects have been built on it.

- Priests detained in reeducation camps are badly treated because they are considered extremely dangerous reactionaries. Criteria for prisoners are to cut and carry back to the camp 4 bamboo trees with sizes pre-prescribed by camp authorities to build houses. The author brings in four of them, but one of them is a little bit smaller. In the evening, camp authorities gather all prisoners in a meeting and punish him, saying: "*because you are a catholic priest, on the coming Sunday you have to go out to cut and bring in 8 bamboo trees. No other prisoners are allowed to give a helping hand..*" Later on, 39 Catholic priests from different camps are moved to the Thanh Cam Camps, Thanh Hoa province where they are put in a small room under strict supervision. They are detained inside days and nights.

- In Northern Vietnam, the Communist authorities strictly control religious activities; censor training curriculum; limit the number of trainees to be admitted and prohibit priest ordaining. As a consequence, priests have very limited knowledge on Catholicism and currently there is a great shortage of priests. In the Bui Chu diocese, only one old priest has to take care of 7 or 8 parishes. In a particular parish, the priest could only conduct a few Masses a year. Because of the restriction policy, some priests are ordained in secret. One of them has been imprisoned for 20 years. Buildings of Bui Chu diocese are in distress.

- The Communists have tried to eliminate the religion, but they are not successful. After they take over the city of Saigon, some soldiers of the North secretly come to see the author asking to attend the Masses. In Long Giao reeducation camp, a Northern soldier secretly performs confessions, plays an intermediary role by asking priests who are running a parish in the Ho Nai area to give bread and wine for the author to conduct Masses at the concentration camp.

It appears that the CPV follows the Polish Communist policy against the religion: In 1960, a Polish Communist delegation led by a politburo member came and visited Hanoi. Ho Chi Minh raised him a question as to how the Communist party of Poland could countrol the country whose people were all Catholics. The Polish replied: *"When the state shows its strength, religion has to back down."*

II. MEASURES AGAINST THE ENENMIES OF THE PROLETARIAT.

All societal classes other than the proletariat such as intellectuals, bourgeois, landlords are enemies of the people and must be liquidated. The purpose of this policy is to achieve a classless society and eliminate potential opposition.

All employees working for the Republic of South Vietnam are enemies. They are sent to reeducation camps. With this spirit, reeducation does not mean what people living in a free society usually think of.

Few months after occupation of the South, the CPV declares that 95% of one million "trainees" have been "graduated" from classes except for 50,000 people who owe blood debts to the Vietnamese people. They have to stay longer in the reeducation camps. Not until the end of 1988, Mai Chi Tho, the minister of Interior admits that the number of long-termed detainees is 500,000.

HOW PRISONERS ARE TREATED?

1) Tortures: There is evidence that the methods of tortures used by the CPV are those taught by the East German Communists. They are more barbarous than those applied in any Communist countries.

2) The Vietnamese communists strictly follow their teacher by implementing the Pavlov theory: conditioning of human body throughout the reeducation

process. Provision of little foods is combined with brainwashing in the hard labor environment and under permanent terrorizing situation. This aims at causing break down of the victim's mental system:

- Forcing prisoners to receive ideological instructions, writing continuous self-criticism during midnights for months, writing and rewriting one's biography about their past activities since birth, about "crimes committed against the people" are major daily activities. In addition, "denunciation" by participants under the sponsorship of the party is encouraged. This takes place during all evening official criticism and self-criticism sessions about one's performance. Permanent shortage of foods providing just enough for prisoners not to die, aims at making prisoners' health deteriorate. Hard labor is included in this process. All of these help destroy prisoners' will to resist.

- Other barbarous methods are also used: using a butcher's knife to cut an appendix; shackling a priest until his feet become spoiled, then using a regular saw to cut them; using pliers to pull out a tooth just because the victim openly states that he is not afraid of the cadre-teachers. Amnesty International reported that the communist cadre raped a female prisoner by using a stick to insert into the victim uterus after her clothes had been taken off. People are not surprised when told about the kangaroo court set up to try landlords during Land Reformed programs in Northern Vietnam before 1954: burying alive a victim's body except for his head and then using a harrow pulled by a water buffalo to cut it off.

- Another method being used is to encourage "prisoners to beat prisoners" to death: a colonel, assembly man Dang Van Tiep and Father Nguyen Huu Le (who happened to survive) for escaping from the camps are examples.Prisoners are also employed as secret informants to provide information against their colleagues. This causes permanent mental tension in prisoners.

I would like to add that inmates who worked clandestinely as agents for the CPV authorities in camps actually did not receive preferences: early release as expected for example. They only received a small award: being allowed staying overnight with their wives or relatives in a separate area when they were permitted to come and visit. Those informers did not know that during the war against the French (1945-1954) so many party members were purged immediately after the French had been defeated, just because they were either intellectual or wealthy. It was these people who had made tremendous sacrifice to the fightings, including but not limited to donations of their wealth, in some case, a portion of their lives to help the party win the war. Furthermore, they had prestige and influence as well, so as to mobilize all segments of the society, especially the peasants into the war. The general populace looked at them as real leaders.

The party from the beginning had never revealed its true identity. It lived under the shell of nationalist movements composed of members of the intellectual and wealthy classes or "bourgeoisie". Therefore, it was not able to persuade them to be involved in the fighting. When the war was won, the party ran into a dilemma: the CPV was a party just for the proletariat. Now, many bourgeois had been adherents to the party. Most of them had held important positions in the party hierarchy. Ho Chi Minh's solution to this problem was to liquidate them. Some 40,000 party members of this category suffered. They were brought before the people's court for trial during the Land Reform program initiated by the party and for having had committed crimes against the people. Most of them were murdered on the spot. The rest was sent to reeducation camps where a number of them still survived until the 1980's.

3) Prisoners' immediate relatives are also affected by the party policy. The PCV states that keeping

the enemies in reeducation camps under these conditions is a humanitarian act. They are supposed to be murdered immediately in the same way as Pol Pot of the Khmer Rouge did to the Cambodian people. Their family members are sent to New Economic zones, located in an isolated and remote area. Their children are not allowed to study beyond the 12th grade. Higher learning education is just for children of the proletariat.

They shall become leaders of the country. Allowing prisoners' children to go to a college means that they would be provided opportunity to become long sleepers in the party ranks. This is a real danger to the party. As a result, children who want to go to a college have to submit to school administration detailed curriculum vitae for the party cell at that institution to check. They will be admitted if their political background is "clean".

III. PERSEVERENCE AND DAILY WORKS OF A MODEL CATHOLIC PRIEST.

On April 28, 1975, the author embarked a naval ship, HQ 001 to flee Vietnam. However, as a Catholic priest he felt guilty leaving his followers behind under an extremely difficult situation. He decided to go home and lived under Communism. After 13 years of imprisonment in different reeducation camps located in jungles in North Vietnam with 11 times of forced displacements, he showed himself a dignified prisoner, without submission to his oppressors. Even as a prisoner he still behaved exactly as a model Catholic priest. He secretly conducted Masses, taught the bible to new converts, helped his faithful gain peace in their minds. Stories as Christ travelled by air during Christmas times, Christ flew over the fences in front of Communist security guards were examples.

I admire Father Que because he did tiny things as a priest, with perseverance, days in days out for 13 years long. As a prisoner of conscience, he enthusiastically provided support to his friends so that the latter could maintain high spirit so as to survive. Anyone of us could deny such daily tiny works done by Father Que are a great thing! A question should be raised as to how he possessed such qualities? I found this right in his answer: *"Faith in God."* He stated that he would voluntarily die in prison as a Catholic priest. With that spirit, he happily lived with a slogan: *"I have a peaceful mind and accept all dangers so that I could overcome all difficulties."* Under that state of mind, he moved forward steadily: doing religious work without forgetting duties of an inmate toward his colleagues and also duties of a citizen toward his country. Love and pardon to others taught by Jesus Christ were also displayed through his daily activities and his thinking reflected the theme.

This memoir covers some good points. The author just describes what was heard and seen chronologically from the times the Communists moved in the city of Saigon, throughout 13 years in 11 reeducation camps. No emotions are involved when he tells the stories. His writing is simple. This truly increases the value of the book.

Briefly, **A Catholic Priest In The Communist Prison** is an other book that contributes to the files of crimes committed by the CPV against the Vietnamese people. Everybody is encouraged to read it in order to understand more about Communism and especially know more about how Faith could interact with the way of living so that people could live peacefully and happily with others.

Dr. Nguyen Van Canh
May, 19, 1998

In reading
The Memoirs of a Priest imprisoned
by the Communists
Some contributing impressions

Authors usually invent very attractive titles to captivate the attention of the readers from the very beginning. Father Dinh Ngoc Que's memoirs is an exception. The title of the memoirs is not resonant, not explosive and yet it does reach the tremendous effect to create emotion and compassion at the readers.

Being an imprisoned priest sounds already tragic, the related prison is of Communist style, and the time spent in prison lasted 13 years! The tittle alone has already succeeded to speak out the barbaric policies of the Communist authorities in Vietnam.

Talking about memoirs is impossible to avoid mentioning the Ego. The French language does have a saying "Le Moi est Haissable" to describe the reluctance when one gets to talk to people about the self-ego.

Here again, Father Que's ego is another exception. It is true that his ego is present in most parts of the book, but such presence is not for bragging but for the harmony with other people. Viewed from that prism, the Ego is no longer detestable and becomes a lovable thing when people read at the very first page of the Memoir: "IF it got to brag then allow me to brag for having the Blessing of God to carry the Calvary in following Him." And the author wrote a sentence enabling the reader to understand the path on which he carries on: "All is the Blessing of God, my past, my present and my future."

In his memoirs, Father Que did not intend to practice literature in terms of polished and academic style. He simply wrote down the truth of 13 years in prison and the maintaining of an iron Faith through so many critical tests. Faith has equipped him with a supernatural strength and said strength covered and dominated the whole 300 pages of his memoirs. And though it was called memoir (relating in principle only events in the past) but the last part of the memoir stated the author's optimistic opinion on the future of Vietnam, optimism also supported by the unwavering Faith of the author.

The memoirs began with a very important decision: he decided to stay in the country when the Communists were reaching the gates of Saigon. Anticipating the difficulties falling on his compatriots, he stayed to share their sufferings. Prison reinforced his conviction that he made the right decision for it empowered him to directly share suffering and disgrace under the yoke of a band of pirates carrying the cosmetic camouflage of revolution and patriotism.

Of course, Father Que did condemn the inhuman policies of the Vietnamese Communists but throughout his memoirs, the reader could not locate any expression of hatred. The memoirs sentenced them with mild images which spoke by themselves eloquently. For example people were so afraid of the Communists that when Saigon changed its masters, they rushed feverishly to buy black fabrics to make clothes ba-ba style. The sky above the Vietnam space was covered with the funeral black color, so gloomy that even the Communists had to ask people to reduce such mournful practice.

For example high placed party members asked Father Que to guide them to come back to the religion. There were party members who requested in secret to make confession. Other party members requested him to celebrate secret Mass. These images and many other things confirmed that his conviction was right: his presence in prison was very helpful to firmly preserve the spirit and morale of those brothers in jail. He also set the example of courage and unyielding to other prisoners so that the illiterate and fanatical cadres could not underestimate them. His light-handed writing style threw into relief the stupid dogmas recited by heart by those party members-rank and file who irony happened to hold the ruling power over the people of Vietnam.

The Communists released Father Que in 1988 but after that he continued to live under surveillance (could not stay in his home at the Redemptorist Congregation), and continued to give secret masses. This situation lasted 5 years when he decided to search for freedom since he believed that at the land of freedom, he could serve his country and compatriots much more effectively.

This important decision once again confirmed that he thought right and did right. For his virtues and supernatural capacity, he was assigned to many important and difficult positions. He fulfilled superbly those functions assigned by his superior.

From this part on, **the remaining pages of the memoirs carried the meaning of a message.** In crowded gatherings of the Vietnamese, in eloquent and highly meaningful sermons, he reminded the Vietnamese in exile (with no religion and social class distinction) not to forget their fatherland and their compatriots, not to let hedonism of foreign material-istic civilization destroying patriotism and the mis-sion to build a Vietnam with no self-anointment and monopoly of power. He sent a common message to the overseas Vietnamese: "The brilliant success is the common success for Vietnam."

The message put special emphasis on the role **of the youths in the building of a Free Vietnam.** The physical Fatherland (mountains, rivers) is still there but the moral and spiritual Fatherland has been broken to pieces by the erroneous and idiotic ruling policies of the primitive dogmatic Marxists. Talking about reconstruction is a hypocritical way and a deliberate trick to avoid the truth. There must be the rebuilding of a Vietnam with no monopoly of self-crown and power in which the citizens must be really respected. **This gigantic task requires the participation of every Vietnamese citizen, among them the youths are the pioneering vanguard force.** The success in education and studies has nothing to be proud of if such education leads only to the search of individual well-being and it merely makes them slaves of foreign materialistic civilization, the civilization that the Russian philosopher in exile Alexander Solzhenitsyn has so rightly condemned as "the civilization of animals." The moral and spiritual Vietnam in shambles needs the contribution of the young generation.

In completing the reading of 13 years in prison, the reader gets the verdict written with sincerity and without hatred. Data reported by the memoirs will provide the evidence to demonstrate to the world that the Vietnamese Communists not only practiced religious persecution but they moreover had the intention to destroy religions.

In the remaining part of the message to

Vietnammeses overseas, the reader got the feeling to read a proclamation admonishing the forward march to destroy an enemy who is even more terrible than the invaders: it is the self-degrading and self debauching in the foreign civilization.

It is honestly correct to conclude that the memoir as it is presented deserves to be received by the readers and compatriots with solemnity and love.

Professor Pham Kim Vinh

Preface

Communism, especially Vietnamese Communism has become a common topic for books, magazines and memoirs of all kinds.

Since 1988, when the Vietnamese Communists made it known to the world that they had abolished the reeducation system, a majority of Southern political prisoners (including me) were released. The rest (approximately 100) were transferred to camp Ham Tan in the South, waiting to be set free gradually as the cadres said. Actually, the Communists did not release the entire remaining prisoners until the end of 1992. Last to be released are four Catholic generals (LMD, LVT, DKG, and TT). Southern political prisoners are military officers, government employees and politicians. After years in jail, they can never forget the nightmares they have gone through since Saigon was "liberated". They truthfully put down in black and white what had happened to them and Vietnam, their homeland. Some of the stories they told, are boiling with rancor and hatred, which requires an immediate reprisal. Some others seem to be fabricated or exaggerated, as they appear incomprehensible to the outsiders. But that is the truth, a naked truth. As living proofs, the authors of those memoirs wrote down their own sufferings and what they had seen with their own eyes. It appears that some spoke highly of themselves. Actually, it is difficult for them to talk about themselves. However, they are forced to do so as the course of events requires.

<u>During the five years in Saigon</u>

I was released in 1988, and like any other priest, not allowed to celebrate Mass and preach in public, or live with the Congregation of the Redemptorists or at other parishes. So, I had to stay at my cousin's house on Dien Bien Phu St.

I am going to tell a small story which had truly happened before I went to live with my cousin.

A fellow priest (father NDT) and I planned to buy a small house. We asked our Superior for permission to live together in it. We chose a house in hamlet 8 where the parish of Mother of Perpetual Help is located. It is a small, old house but we can make it livable at a repair cost of about 2 or 3 teals of gold. With our superior's permission and after the selling price was settled, I represented father NDT and reported to the city that we would move to our new house in hamlet 8, on Ky Dong St, District 3, Saigon. A cadre stepped out to see me. After a moment of thinking, he said: "As this matter should be considered carefully, we will answer you tomorrow at 4:00 p.m."

The following day, I was present at the public security office at 4 p.m. as scheduled. Five then ten minutes passed without the cadre appearing. Being impatient, I went to a nearby office and said to a cadre: "Sir, I have an appointment with cadre L. at 4 o'clock this afternoon, and until now, he has not arrived yet. Call him for me, please!" Just at that time, cadre L. arrived. He said in a loud voice: "Mr. Que, your situation is very complicated." While I still did not understand what he meant, he continued: "As priests, you are not permitted to live together. According to the policy of the party and the revolutionary government, two priests are not allowed to live together in the house at Ky Dong St, hamlet 8. You'd better find another place and let us know."

Unable to believe my ears, I said aloud: "Two people are not allowed to live together? What in the world is a law! Really, I can never find such a law anywhere else. Living by myself, how can I get help if I happen to have a sudden stomachache during the night?"

At my dissatisfaction, cadre L. stressed each of his words, saying: "It's the policy of the party and the government. You must comply with the law. If you don't try to find a legal place to live soon, we will find it for you." Upon these words, he left. I turned back, thinking to myself: Priests are their targets of hate. I must be careful not to let them select for me if I want to live a decent life. In the North, they have done it to a number of priests already. Thinking so, I made up my mind to go to my cousin. And the following day, I had my name registered in the census book at once. Since that time, I became detained so to speak in one place, as I had to report to the quarter's office each time I wanted to go far from home or to be absent from home for a few days. What a wonderful way of controlling people!

As a recently-released prisoner, not allowed to truthfully live a priest's life due to all kinds of limitations and enforcement, I thought to myself: The Communists have tortured me and wanted me dead. But, thank God! I am still alive. Before going to jail, I had been a priest. In jail, I was a priest, and now released from jail, I am still a priest. During the days in jail, I did my best to assist my friends spiritually as a priest's mission requires (and I did it all in the dark to avoid the watchful eyes of the atheists.) Who can forbid me to do my duties as a priest now, while I am enjoying some freedom outside prison? I have believed and still believe in the wisdom of the Holy Spirit. He always stays with me as a guiding light for all of my activities.

Thinking so, I did not hurry to start my public life.

At the Congregation of the Redemptorists in Saigon, I served as a chaplain for the brothers, teaching them theology and religious doctrine, enabling them to become teachers themselves, and if possible, to become deacons for the service of the Holy Church.

One of them, brother L.C. Khap, was allowed to continue his theological studies and was ordained to the priesthood in 1997. Thanks be to the Lord!

I accepted to be an associate for the novitiate

master, preaching to those who retreated for the initiation rite into religious life, or for making vows, and teaching the novices Mariology every Saturday throughout the year. I was very much interested in teaching this subject as I had a chance to proclaim the glory of my Holy Mother who had been to me a great source of consolation when I was in Communist prison.

I also assisted the brothers in need of taking a vow again or making a vow for life, helped them get ready for deacon-ship and served as a spiritual guide for those who came to me in private.

<u>My apostolic activities outside</u>
<u>the Congregation</u>

While in Vietnam, I preached during monthly retreats to the sisters of St. Paul de Chartres at 6, Cuong De Blvd, Saigon, to the sisters of St. Vincent de Paul at 38 Tu Xuong Ave, Saigon and to the lovers of the Cross Phu Xuan, on Le Van Sy lane, Saigon. I often celebrated Mass for the above-mentioned convents, especially for Saint Paul clinic (now Dien Bien Phu Hospital)

At the Mother of Perpetual Help Parish run by the Congregation of the Redemptorists, the Superior permitted me to secretly reestablish Legio Mariae and preside over weekly meetings of the sub groups as I was not allowed to work in public.

At the first meeting of the association, there were only seven or eight brothers and sisters. The feast of Mary's Immaculate Conception on Dec 8, 1989 marked the opening of the association. When I left for the United States (Nov 1, 1993), the number of members swelled rapidly and the association was in full swing. Until now (1998) there are 8 or 9 groups altogether, with over 100 active members and approximately 1000 sympathizers and sponsors. It is really a mighty army under the command of Mary. The association is still in permanent contact with me, and I always cooperate with them in their apostolic activities. The association has survived difficult times. Thanks be to God! They work for God and He will take care of them; they work for Mary, and She will protect and help them.

The lay apostolate realized by the association of Legio Mariae Curia I reestablished at the Mother of Perpetual Help Parish has revived other organizations in neighboring parishes and influenced even Senatus of Saigon favorably. Following are some of their achievements while I was still in Saigon, worth mentioning for the glory of God.

A retired Communist cadre converting to Catholicism

Through the Legio Mariae's activities, a high ranking Communist Cadre, over 40 party years old, converted to Catholicism. I had the honor to come to his house to baptize him, perform the sacrament of confirmation upon him, legitimate his marriage and give the Holy Communion to him and his family members during the Thanksgiving Mass.

During baptism, I asked him:

- What do you ask for from the Holy Church?

- Monsignor, please, baptize me so that I can serve God, the Party and the government more effectively.

The ritual continued slowly. Before pouring water over his head, I asked him once more:

- Sir, do you really want me to baptize you?

He answered in an affirmative voice:

- Monsignor! I ask you to baptize me so that I have enough strength to serve God, the Party and the government.

I then baptized him and performed on him all the liturgies I had mentioned before.

Everything happened satisfactorily. The Legio's members and his family organized a simple food party in his honor. His folks planned to bring food to his bed, as he was too ill and tired. But surprisingly, he insisted on eating together with others, especially on sitting beside "Monsignor" to talk with him. During the meal, he kept talking and smiling easily just like a child. He felt really peaceful and relaxed, as he had become a God's child. He kept repeating again and again: "I have never been happier in my life. Thanks to Monsignor! Thanks to brothers and sisters! Please, don't forget to come again and again to see me!"

Later, I come to know that after being baptized, he changes noticeably. Before, he was a hot-tempered person, often abusing his family members and cursing the party and the revolution for having robbed him of the rewards of his labor. Having followed the Revolution for several years and achieved so much for the party, he retired due to old age and poor health, living on a meager monthly pension of some ten thousand piasters. Now, after baptism, he becomes a good-natured man, pleasant to his family, winning the esteem of everybody. Thanks be to God!

<u>Another achievement by Legio Mariae</u>

It is the story of another retired cadre. He was also over 40 party years old, living at the same time with Mr. Nguyen Van Linh and Uncle Ho. He was seriously ill and according to his family members, not far from death.

He was a Southerner regrouping in the North. When Saigon was "liberated," he returned to the South, lucky enough to meet his family members again. He used to be a Catholic, but he had left God to follow uncle Ho and the revolution. When he was ill, he was well attended by his family. One of his children was surprisingly, a member of Legio Mariae in the Mother of Perpetual Help parish. She attended daily meetings and often reported on her father's situation. I accepted her invitation to come over to their house to attend to her father's spiritual needs.

The following afternoon, I went to his bedside and talked to him about God's mercy. I was talking and counseling him when I saw tears well up in his eyes. I then bent down over his face and consoled him: "God died and rose again for our salvation. He is always ready to forgive all those who come to him with a repentant heart and give them life and peace."

I talked and talked for a rather long moment. Finally I asked him: "Do you want to come back to God, sir?" After a few seconds, he opened his eyes, looked at me and nodded in agreement. My heart was overwhelmed with joy. I then helped him confess his sins and receive the last rituals. After that, I blessed him for the absolution of all his sins.

Before leaving, I advised his family to take care of him during the last hours of his life. He came back to God, that very night.

His family members grieved over the loss of their loved one; however, they gained more faith in God as they had witnessed his conversion.

Since he was a high-ranking party member, visitors from the central government came in great number. Aware of the situation, I told his family that I would celebrate the funeral Mass at their home only. The Mass started at 8:00 a.m., and the burial service at 10:00 a.m.

That day, while sharing God's words, I talked about the permanent residence of man in Heaven and about this temporary life on earth. Whatever happens, everyone must die, at last. Blessed are those who can come back to their Creator after death. My eulogy was rather long as I had a chance to implicitly preach to the Communist cadres who had come in great number for the Mass.

After celebrating the Mass and performing all the necessary rituals for the dead person, I said good-bye to the grieving family and stealthily went home through the back door.

Later on, his family let me know that many cadres had asked: "Who is the preacher during the funeral mass? He is very eloquent." I prayed to God that all the Communists present that day might be able to come back to their "root" like the dead person.

<u>During the First Five Years in the United States.</u>

The airplane carrying me landed on the Los Angeles international airport at noontime, Jan. 12, 1993. The Vice provincial overseas, some fathers and brothers of the Congregation, and a number of relatives and friends greeted me at the airport. I received fresh bouquets, warm embraces and tight handshakes from the dear ones I had not met for a long time. Everybody rejoiced at seeing me. As for me, my joy was not complete as a part of my heart was still in Vietnam. That day, the rain poured down on California.

Is it because God blesses me? I asked myself. O Lord! I put all my confidence in You. My future is in your hand. I am only a humble creature. Please, protect and guide me always!

We left the airport and went by car to the Congregation of the Redemptorists at the city of Long Beach where a reception party was held in my honor. Everyone was happy at the meeting. I tried to share the happy moment with my brothers, friends and relatives.

After the reception, at the designation of the Vice provincial (Rev. Chau Xuan Bau), I headed for the Congregation of the Redemptorists at the city of Baldwin Park, Ca.

The following morning, my younger brother Dinh Ngoc Thu came to take me to the city of Santa Ana. He introduced me to USCC and this agency agreed to sponsor me. Since I did not want to live with my brother, he rented for me a furnished room at his son-in-law's house on condition that I had to share a restroom with the family. USCC paid for room and board for me including other utilities such as electricity, water, phone, etc. I accepted to live at subsistence level just like any other H.O member who was living on government subsidy.

I was eligible to 8-month period of subsidy. However, just two months later, I was able to enjoy SSI and Medicaid benefits thanks to my old age.

When I went to apply for old age benefits, I was

lucky enough to meet with a Vietnamese social worker. As soon as I told my name, he reacted favorably, saying: "I have known you before, father! Especially I have heard about your activities in Communist camps. You have done a lot to help the prisoners. Now, our responsibility is to help you in return." Upon those words, he turned on his computer and typed on it what are best for me.

Life often alternates between fortune and misfortune. Misfortune? Yes, I have experienced a lot of them. As for fortune, however small it is, I always consider it as a fringe benefit, a blessing God has bestowed upon me to comfort and support me.

I shared room for a few months only. After that, I went to live with my younger sister and her child, and continued to do what were necessary for the settlement of a new life in America. The first thing I needed was to have a car as a means of transportation. To depend on others, even on my brothers or sisters might cause some inconvenience, I thought. Therefore in less than one month, I succeeded in getting a used Toyota Cressida, just 60,000 miles old, still in rather good condition. I began to study traffic rules and driving codes and practice with the car I just bought. It took me only two weeks to get the driver's license. The following day, with my "new" car, I got onto the freeway and headed for my Congregation at once. I felt happy, so did everybody. All the paper work and planning for the settlement being done in two months, I began to contact people and go preaching to the Catholic communities in Santa Ana, Westminster, Garden Grove and many others in the United States. Wherever I went, besides pastoral duties, I tried to promote a movement of "young people for a better Vietnam."

Those activities helped me adapt to the new life more quickly.

Back to my Congregation

During the first few months, I went around and worked so passionately that I forgot my duty to come back to my Congregation and live with my colleagues. What will happen, is bound to happen.

In May, 1993, the Vice provincial (Rev. Chau Xuan Bau) phoned me and went to see me at my younger sister's place. For convenience, we agreed to meet at Nha Trang restaurant in Westminster, where we had lunch together and talked about many topics concerning our Congregation overseas. Our conversation in the restaurant lasted almost 4 hours (from 11 a.m. to 3 p.m.)

As a result, I was appointed Superior of the Vietnamese Redemptorist Monastery, at Baldwin Park, CA on July 16th, 1993.

Three months later, I was in charge of the St. Joseph Community at West Covina, CA.

At the same time, I was appointed Novice Master for the school year 94-95.

On May 25th, 1996, I was again appointed Novice Master for the school year 96-97.

As a Superior, an associate pastor and a Novice

Master, I must be wise and subtle enough to deal reasonably with both internal and external affairs, as those three positions weighed heavy on my shoulders.

The St. Joseph Community in particular required a lot of my effort and sacrifice. To speed up the progress of the Community, I solidified the executive committee and promoted the activities of various lay apostolate groups (the coalition of the Sacred Heart, the Catholic mothers.) I formed a group of Eucharistic Children (with 300 members at the opening ceremony), stressed the importance of a parish-choir, considering it as a center of activities for the young. I also organized Vietnamese courses for the children, regardless of religion to maintain the Vietnamese culture.

As a Redemptorist, I tried to practice the spirit of my Congregation whose mission is to serve God and His people, and to testify to the Good News. I placed an emphasis on religious instruction for the catechumens, preparing them for baptism and confirmation. My purpose was to improve the Community so that everybody could fit in the new situation.

As a result, the St. Joseph Community became more unified and changed noticeably for the better.

I have never been unemployed in my life. Jobs come to me as blessings from Heaven. With that concept in mind, I do my best to realize God's will. Though limited in skills and virtues, when receiving my superior's order, I feel braced with the Holy Spirit, ready to accept sacrifice for the sake of my Congregation.

When I served as a Novice Master for the first time (94-95), four brothers (Ha, Son, Trung, Viet) took vows.

During my second term as a Novice Master, three others (Thach, Dong, Long) took vows.

After three years of service as a superior and an associate pastor, a major shuffle of personnel took place in the Congregation. Just when I reached the age of 70, two loads being lifted off my shoulders, I only served as a Novice Master. Thanks be to the Lord!

I think some day, even my role of a Novice Master will be replaced by another person, more qualified than I. I am now waiting for the eternity.

What is left for me? That is the basic question of my life?

I firmly believe that there is only Love of God remaining.

May this God-given love erase all my sins, mistakes and defects and turn what I have done all my life for God and His people into a fragrant bouquet before God's presence to proclaim his glory forever.

I am taking off this school year (97-98) as there are no more novices.

Before the new millennium jubilee arrives, to mark the 10th anniversary of my release from prison (88-98) and to realize the wish of my friends who want me to share my experiences with them when living under the Communist regime, particularly during the 13 years in prison called "reeducation camp", I accept to write **Memoirs of a Priest imprisoned in the Communist Prison**.

In my memoirs, I would like to speak out on what I have experienced with my friends and done with them and for them, helping them maintain their human dignity, whereas the Communists called us "prisoners" and sought every means to vilify and insult us. In spite of that, we tried to keep our faith, and behave as theists in front of those who call themselves atheists, but deep inside, still fear death and God's punishment, and never stop worrying about the presence of the theists.

I will do my best to realize your wish. Would you please pardon me, my friends, in case I am not able to come up to the level of your expectation.

Baldwin Park
Sept. 23, 1997

I. A LIFE-CHANGING DECISION

Months before the event of April 30th,1975, my cousin, an employee of the Vietnamese Consulate in San Francisco, California, in charge of Vietnamese students in the U.S., wrote to me, affirming that South Vietnam would fall into the Communists' hands as planned according to current American global policy. He advised me to leave Vietnam for the U.S at once. He stated the reason saying: "As a government employee under the regime of South Vietnam, you cannot live with the Communists." Listening to VOA and BBC Radios, I knew that after successive falls of the Highlands, Quang Tri, Hue, Da nang, Nha Trang ... Communist troops with armored tanks and heavy artillery were approaching Saigon. Rockets fell everywhere, especially in Tan Son Nhut area. People were in complete confusion. Armies of the

Republic of Vietnam were thrown into total chaos due to lack of leadership. President Thieu hopelessly appealed to the U.S. for military aid.

I phoned to general T.D.T in the operation Bureau, General Staff to get informed of the current military situation and tried to keep permanent contact with the Headquarters of the capital special military zone, for the ever-changing situation in Saigon, Cho-lon, Gia dinh.

At that moment, our troops' spirit still remained high. They pledged to fight to the end, but as their leaders showed signs of let-up, any effort on their part came to nothing. Bad rumors were spreading like wildfire. People in the streets were talking about the change of hands in the government, about president Thieu's departure, about G.I's and civilian employees ready to leave Vietnam in 48 hours.

At that time, general B.D.D and I decided to flee as my cousin had advised. On April 28th, I went home to say "good bye" to my family-members and relatives and get ready to pack. I embarked a naval ship No. 001, willing to share a cabin reserved for officers. Captain H. and I agreed on the date of departure. Another option for me was to fly by helicopter from the U.S. embassy straight to the 7th fleet in the Pacific Ocean. I could not get to sleep that night. My head tense with thoughtfulness, my heart heavy with remorse. As a priest, I felt very guilty. The priest is a shepherd and the shepherd has no right to leave his sheep alone especially in difficult times. A good shepherd must sacrifice his life to save his sheep from the wolves. I thought to myself, am I as good a shepherd as the one mentioned by Jesus in the gospel? If I go abroad for a relatively easy life, I am considered too selfish to be a good shepherd, which contradicts the ideal of a priest. Thinking so, I decided to stay in order to share joys and sorrows with my brothers and sisters. The word "Fiat" brought peace to my mind.

That morning, I got up early and headed for my younger brother's house on Le Van Duyet St. to let him know I had changed my mind and decided to stay.

Back to my Congregation, I phoned to the general, my friend, telling him I needed to see him badly. He invited me to come right away, as a meeting was going to be held at his headquarters. He welcomed me to his office and we had a private talk behind closed doors. I let him know my decision to stay. The news surprised him. He said in a voice shaking with emotion: "You are a priest. You can perform your pastoral duties wherever you go. What will happen to us while living abroad without a priest's spiritual guidance. We really need you, father." I tried to console him: "General, you still have a family to take care. You've got to go, especially for your children to have a better future.You will certainly enjoy more freedom in foreign countries. It is also easy to find a priest, too. My situation is different. As a shepherd, I cannot leave my sheep at this critical moment. I feel very guilty if I leave. Please, go in peace with your family. Let us keep one another in prayers so that each of us can fulfill our own duties." I then said "good bye" to him and went home.

I did not even know the day when the general and his family went.

The 29th of April was an extremely tense day. Saigon was in chaos. The city was echoed with the chopping sounds of helicopters carrying refugees mixed with the explosion of Communist rockets falling everywhere. Saigon streets were jammed with refugees. A number of my fellow priests (chaplains from neighboring cities) and I ran around, trying to do whatever we can to help people such as providing them with food and shelter.

Early in the morning, April 30th, a phone-call from the capital special military zone let me know that our troops had stopped the communists from invading Tan Son Nhut airport. It was a very good piece of news. Everybody felt encouraged.

But at 10 a.m. When general Duong Van Minh declared to surrender unconditionally, the capital of Saigon was left open to the invaders. The news left me dazed like being lightning-struck. It seemed as if the sky had been collapsed and a black heavy pall had fallen all over Saigon. The Southerners seemed to faint. Nobody talked. Everyone sighed deeply in sadness.

To lose the country is to lose everything, I thought. What will happen when the Communists take Saigon and the whole nation is lost to them. Everybody looked extremely sad and perplexed.

I lost two jeeps and a van that very night. They had been stolen by certain "revolutionary of the 25th hour."

In a situation like "fishing in troubled waters", I'd better stay indoors. So I shut myself in a private room on Ky Dong st. for a whole week. I could not risk my life going out at the time when everything was in limbo, and nothing was settled, especially when one could not even tell friend from enemy.

After a week, I obeyed my superior to celebrate Sunday Mass scheduled at 7:30 a.m. in the church of the Mother of perpetual help. That was the first Mass I celebrated in public after Saigon had been "liberated".

Everybody was surprised when they saw me at the altar. They thought I had escaped on a helicopter parking in the church-grounds for a pilot to lift his family members on the morning of April 30th. After the Mass, a great number of people flocked to the reception room to greet me. I began to realize that my decision to stay was really right. May God help me.

During a week of hiding, there were two facts I can never forget.

Fact I: A ghost-town

At around noontime, on May first, a fellow priest and I ventured out in disguise. We rode a Honda around Saigon, Cho lon, Gia dinh to visit the places

I had served as a chief chaplain in the Capital special military zone. I could not believe my eyes. Saigon had become a ghost-town. It was noontime, yet, offices, businesses and markets were still tightly closed.

The streets were littered with abandoned military uniforms. My heart ached at the sight of three-red-stripe yellow flags of the Republic of Vietnam thrown in tatters on the streets and in waste baskets. Some people were brave enough to go collecting those torn pieces of clothing. They tried to load their rickshaws or wheelbarrows with those military stuffs and brought them home. They might be wise to act their own way, I thought.

Once in a while appeared a Molotova driven by a communist soldier. He drove recklessly in every direction, ignoring traffic regulations. We had the feeling he was driving in the jungle during an operation. As he won the war, he thought he had the privilege to do whatever he pleased and that his priorities must be respected. When we came to the intersection of Hai Ba Trung St. and Phan Dinh Phung St. (now is called Dien Bien Phu), we saw a military vehicle crashing against an electric pole. We did not know if the driver could servive the accident to savor the fruits of his victory. So was Saigon; but Cho Lon was no better, and Gia Dinh was even worse. Both of us went on and on in silence for two hours, observing everything around us. Finally, we stopped at a road-inn in Thu Duc. We ate a quick snack and returned home with the image of a ghosttown weighing heavy on our minds. Everything happened just like it was yesterday.

Fact 2: A city in mourning

A few days after the liberation, an unusual scene appeared. Without giving notice to one another, men, women, especially young girls were trying to dress in black to such a degree that all the black fabrics were sold out in the market. Loose black shirts (ao ba ba den) and rubber sandals were becoming an instant fad. When young girls went out, they did not care to wear flashy gorgeous clothes. People did so on purpose to mourn the death of South Vietnam, or was it just a pure coincidence? Nobody knew.That strange fashion was spreading so wide and so fast that in an article, "Liberated Saigon News" voiced their concern, advising people to get rid of black clothes for fear of damaging the beauty of Saigon, an emerald of the Orient. The revolutionary newspaper also encouraged the public to be happy and dress well to beautify the city. This mourning fashion lasted for a while before fading away naturally.

When general Duong Van Minh declared to surrender the Communists, Saigon became shrouded with a pall of black cloud. After Saigon fell into the hands of the Communists, everybody dressed in black, as a sign of mourning the death of South Vietnam, and also as an expression of deep sorrows on the part of the losers.

Seeing me celebrate Mass in public, many parishioners went home, informing their friends and relatives that father Que was still at 38 Ky Dong St., and the rumor of his escape was not true. Knowing I was still in Saigon, the new Chief of quarter 12, district 10 where my office had been located, did not hesitate to invite me to come over. There must be something, I thought to myself. Once I have decided to stay, for my friends' sake, I should not live in hiding. Instead, I have to continue my public life and do whatever I can to help people. Upon that idea, I went ahead and made an appointment with the quarter chief at 2:00 p.m. at his office.

I used to travel by car and have a driver of my own. Now, without that comfortable means of transportation, I volunteered to walk to the quarter-chief's office. I must however use an umbrella because it took me 20 minutes to get to his office under the hot sun. At my sight, the quarter chief went to the door to greet me. He shook my hand heartily, saying: "I'm so happy to see you here. It's right for you to stay. Don't worry, father! You have done nothing wrong. Now, you should get involved in social activities. I need your cooperation to improve the condition of our quarter. I will provide all the necessary means for you."

Truly, I had nothing to worry about at that time. The new quarter chief is the person I know well, a former low-ranking officer of the military police. His platoon used to station right at the gate of the headquarters of the Capital special military zone. His family members pass by my church every day. All his children are Tinh Than high school students and I am the school principal and director.Strangely enough, nobody knows he is a local Communist spy. When Saigon fell, he revealed himself and was appointed quarter chief.

He invited me to sit down on a chair and have a cup of Chinese tea. We exchanged many ideas concerning the activities in the quarter. I promised to support his efforts. After about two-hour talk, I went back to my residence at 38 Ky Dong St.

The Communists are so clever at disguising themselves, I thought to myself. Two Communist spies have worked right at my office. I did not send them to the battlefield, hopefully to save their lives. Instead, I employed them as construction workers for my new chapel in the special military zone of the capital. I have held them in high esteem, and they have done their best to help me in return.

I went over to inspect Tinh Than high school and the chapel, the following day. Meeting a captain in the schoolyard, I introduced myself I was the principal, director of the school and told him my intention of seeing the commander of the troops. He answered with a smile: "It's me. What do you want?" "Captain," I answered, "according to a radio announcement, schools should be open as usual. Therefore, I would like you to move your troops elsewhere so that my school can continue its activities."

He pointed to the area behind the school, saying: "I've just got the order to move there in two days."

I thanked the captain and asked his permission to go around to inspect my school. School-papers and students' grade reports were torn away and thrown in piles on the floor. The school safe-box had been prized wide-open with nothing in it. Upstairs, almost all the windows had been used by soldiers as firewood for cooking. The restrooms on both sides of the school building looked messy and gave out an offensive odor. Before that awful sight, my heart sank at the thought of bad consequences of the revolution our young generation would have to suffer in the future.

In the evening, the quarter-chief called me to join an 9:00 p.m. conference. I was invited to preside over the meeting. We heard the chief lavish praise on the victory of revolution, confirming that the revolution would bring abundant food and clothing to the whole nation, that paradise would be real, right here on earth. He spoke passionately on and on. Everybody held his breath and listened attentively to every of his single words. But when he stopped to ask for input from the audience, nobody said a word. An uncomfortable silence reigned over the conference room, which forced the chief to adjourn ahead of schedule.

After everybody had gone, the quarter-chief came to me and said: "I know, you have no means of transportation now. We don't want you to live far

66

from us. So, I have reserved for you a R4 van and a villa near your school, where colonel G. used to live. Remember to come over tomorrow to take the keys for the car and the house as well." I thanked him for his kindness while feeling a little bit uneasy about his unusually nice attitude. After moving into the house and receiving the van, I destroyed one section of the dividing wall between my house and the school, leaving a connecting passage for both sides. At the same time, I had a gate raised for the school and the church to use in common as an exit passing by my residence to Le Van Duyet boulevard, without having to go via the general staff.

Now, my students and the church-goers could share the same gate. It was so convenient, exactly as I wished. Many thanks to the quarter-chief for his care. From then on, I was able to organize very often activities for students and various groups and celebrate Mass every evening, especially on Sundays.

A soldier, the Mother of Perpetual Help's Child
During the first Sunday Mass after the revolution, the church was full. I reserved some pews for a number of revolutionary soldiers who came to "watch" the Mass and listen to religious songs of the South. Nobody knew if they were Catholics or not. We did not dare to ask, anyway. That day, I felt very free to share the words of God with parishioners. When the time of the Holy Communion came,

I requested those who were not Catholics to remain at their seats, and not to receive the Communion. The soldiers seemed very docile. None of them disobeyed me.

After Mass, I got into the sacristy. When I walked out, I saw three soldiers wearing *Nón-cối* (a round-topped hat popular in French colonial time) come to me. There must be something wrong, I thought. I tried to calm down and asked:

- Who are you looking for?

- We want to see you, father.

The way they addressed me, really surprised me.

- Please, follow me to the schoolyard, I said.

The church of the Capital special Military zone has a second floor. It was just 80 percent finished. A marble altar should be added to be complete. The inauguration day was scheduled on August 15th, 1976, the Assumption of Mary, patron saint of the Church.

We stopped in the schoolyard and continued our conversation.

- What can I do for you, I asked?

- We are very happy to attend the Holy Mass today. This is our first time since we left the North seven years ago. We need the sacrament of reconciliation.

It was a wonderful surprise for me. Knowing for sure they were Catholics, I asked:

- What diocese in the North do you belong to?

- Diocese of Bui Chu, father, they answered.

I continued with an inquisitive voice:

- Seven years have passed since you left the North and lived in the jungle ever since, with continuous military movements going on. How have you been able to practice your religion during those years?

- When meeting together and knowing we were Catholics, we tried to encourage one another to say prayers as a way of practicing religion. We did it in secret, because if cadres in our group know, we would be in trouble.

During the conversation, one of them reached into his pocket for a worn-out wallet and took from it an image of the Mother of Perpetual Help. The picture appeared to be torn to shreds all around and fading in color except Mary's face still clear. He showed me the picture, saying:

- Before my departure to the South, my mother gave me this picture and said: "I don't know what will happen to you on the way South. Remember to keep this treasure with you always and pray for her perpetual protection during the perilous journey." Following my mother's advice, I say the "Hail Mary" every day and have survived the bombardment of B52 several times. I remember one special time when a bomb-shred landed on my breast-pocket, I got unconscious and fell down. When regaining consciousness and finding the picture of Mary still in the pocket, I realized Mother had saved me.

The story touched me deeply. Most parishioners in Northern Vietnam are familiar with the miraculous image of the Mother of Perpetual Help and her temple at Thai Ha hamlet in Hanoi run by the Redemptorists. I asked them:

- You've just said you want to confess your sins, but have you examined yourselves carefully?

- We are ready, father.

I then brought them into my office where I performed the sacrament of reconciliation upon each of them. We are often told that most Catholics lose their faith easily under the persecution of the Communists. But from my experience while in prison, I come to understand that the more one is persecuted and tortured, the more one sticks to God, and the harder one's faith is tested, the stronger it becomes. As a result, many more people come to God.

I then assured them:

- You can come for the Mass and receive the Holy Communion tomorrow or this coming Saturday.

I did see them come up and receive the Communion the following day.

When the Mass was over, they asked me for a hymnbook. To them, religious songs of the South are so wonderful.

Besides school duties, I also cooperated with the quarter chief in social activities such as having my students clean up public areas in nearby streets. As a school principal, I was invited to a meeting on education, on the implementation of Marxist-Leninist ideas upheld by the Party and Uncle Ho. The lecturer talked like a parrot. The meeting was so boring and tiring. Yet, we were forced to attend.

During the first few weeks after the Communist victory, the atmosphere in the city was getting more and more oppressive. Nobody dared to go out, for fear that Saigon would be bathed in blood. It was rumored that in order to pay tribute to Uncle Ho and the Communist party, girls must marry the war-invalids to repay them for their sacrifice for the revolution, that if a girl refused manual work, her red or rose-painted fingernails would be removed.

Street robbery was so rampant that the revolutionary government had to resort to force and shoot violators on the spot.

Was Saigon bathed in blood?

No, Saigon was not bathed in blood. It was only a rumor.

After the fall of Saigon, only secret killings and grenade explosions took place. Communist soldiers were ordered never to go out alone for fear of the angry public's reprisal. No girls were to marry soldiers or had red-painted fingernails removed. During my visit to a boarding girl-school, the principal complained: "It's quite a problem caused to me by the girls, father! Everyone of them keep in reserve two or three bottles of aspirin." Understanding their situation, I just smiled.

Saigon was not bathed in blood.
With the policy of re-education,
however, it was even worse than a blood-bath

The South Vietnam "liberated" as they often call it, was put under a strict control and governed by a system of unspeakable cruelty. It is the reeducation policy that causes most fear and horror to all. Hundreds of thousands of Southerners including military officers, government employees, civilians... must report for reeducation. It is certainly the most brutal, deceitful, tricky scheme of all, a devilish invention known only to the Communists.You'd rather go through a onetime blood-bath than die slowly in remote mountainous areas and suffer in a health-threatening environment under extremely unseasonable weather conditions while deprived of all civil rights and treated as animals. They use every means they can possibly imagine to exploit you physically, and yet, ironically consider you lucky, just because your life is spared by the "so-called" leniency and benevolence of the Revolution. One of the biggest mistakes the Communists have ever made is to waste the most precious human resources of the nation when they send so many technicians, specialists, professionals and intellectuals to the jungle for labor. Even worse, their secret plan as we come to know it while in prison, is to abolish ""three generations" by forcing entire families including parents, wives, husbands, children and even grand children to leave their homes in the South and move far up

North to "new economic zones" such as Thanh Phong, Yen bai, Hoang Lien Son... with no hope of return. The Communists also reserved for us, Catholic priests, a detention-camp named "Heaven Gate" in Cao Bang. Seven or eight chaplains were the first to be there before China gave Vietnam a lesson. We met them later at camp Thanh Cam, Thanh Hoa in an area formerly called Ly Ba So.

The Communists do contradict themselves. They are claiming they have liberated the nation, but actually they do nothing but destroy it. To them, the Party comes first. They think they have an exclusive right to love the country, and their political system is unique. How can Vietnam be developed and civilized under such an authoritarian regime? The fact is that in the North from 1954 and in the South from 1975 till now the Communists have failed miserably in everything, leaving Vietnam lag far behind neighboring countries. They must be held accountable to the nation for that and stand the trial of history. Nobody can understand how miserable we were and how badly we had been treated while in reeducation camps.

Living with the Communists cadres, we come to know the type of person they are and the social class they belong to. Do they truly represent the Party and the regime? We understand better than anybody else while in prison, the true nature of the Communists and their revolutionary ideas. Do they really love the country while putting the Communist

Party on top of everything even at the expense of the nation. The better we understand them, the harder it is for us to accept the way they govern the country.

I am classified as an extreme reactionary who mistrusts Uncle Ho and the Communist Party. I know this because I happen to read in the 3-year report about me the following words: an extremely reactionary element.

The axiom "Man proposes but God disposes" rings true all the time. We cannot go against God's will. We certainly don't live forever, we know this is true and time will prove it.

Toward the end of May, newspapers, especially the Liberated Saigon journal and Saigon Radio announced that all the military officers, government employees and politicians of South Vietnam must report for reeducation.

I followed the order. On June 15, 1975, together with two fellow priests (Rev. NVT and Rev. NDT) each of us got on a rickshaw and headed for Tabert School to register for reeducation. Each of us must advance 25,000 piasters for food. We brought along clothes and necessities just enough for one month as they had said (as everybody knows later, one month turns out to be 13 years.)

"One doesn't like what one doesn't know." We have to understand the new regime in order to like it and adapt to it more easily. It is only for one month, I thought to myself, I will try my best to study hopefully to serve the country better. The quarter-chief himself had also let me know in advance and assured me: "You too, have to report for reeducation. It is only for one month. After that, you will be back to help us."

His sympathetic words seemed to calm me down. But how can we know what will happen in the future.

II. ACCEPTING TO DIE IN PRISON

Tabert School, Saigon
On June 15, 75, I went to Tabert school in Saigon to report. My two fellow priests (Rev. NVT and Rev. NDT) and I were assigned to a resting place upstairs. As soon as we entered the room, we were greeted by an unpleasant odor from excrement and urine all over the place.

Our first humiliating job was to clean the filthy room for the night. We were not surprised because we were told that after invading Saigon, revolutionary troops had stationed here.

We tried to console one another: "Don't worry! It is only for one month."

After the clean-up, we spread a sheet of nylon on the floor to sit on and wait for dinner. We waited and waited till 9:00 p.m. before we knew that those who reported, that afternoon which was the last day, had to bring their own food. Luckily, before going, we took along a couple of loaves of lean pork meat and some bread. We ate in a hurry, so that we could sleep early, waiting for the following day. The hard cold floor did not bother us. Too tired, we lay down and slept easily after that. At midnight, we were suddenly awakened by the resounding sound of a whistle. Everybody looked bewildered. What's happening, we asked ourselves. We did not know anything until a cadre came ordering: "Hurry up! Pack your stuff! Go down to the schoolyard and get in line!" My two colleagues and I reminded each other to stick together, hopefully to travel in the same vehicle and live at the same place. We planned to carry out this idea to the end. And we had succeeded with this plan. During 13 years in prison, we always traveled together, lived together, were released and came home together, at the same time. This is really a God's blessing, a miracle, we believe. So we tried to support one another in everything.

Down in the schoolyard, we saw many familiar faces. We were formed in groups of 20, so that each vehicle could accommodate one group. There were many cadres dressed in yellow, wearing *nón-cối* (a round-topped hat used in French colonial time) with a gun in hand. They appeared ready to take us to the execution ground. They ordered silence through a loudspeaker. A cadre with a pistol at his waist and a brown leather bag in hand (he might be a leader) raised his voice through the loudspeaker: "Listen, you, the elements of a fake army and a puppet government! You must absolutely stay with your group and follow your warden. Anyone who dare to resist or cause trouble, shall be severely punished or shot on the spot."

Each group was escorted by a warden out of Tabert school to one of Molotovas ready on both sides of the street. Everywhere were armed soldiers, ready to guard against any mishap which might occur. We climbed into our vehicle and sat on the floor, facing forward. Canvases all around began to fall, leaving us in total darkness. The air inside the vehicle was getting oppressive. We wondered where they were going to take us. When all the vehicles started moving, one of us tried to look out through a hole in the canvas, but saw nothing in the dark.

Long Giao

After about 2 hours of travelling, the convoy stopped. It was around 3:00 a.m. We broke into small groups, and a separate area was designated to each group. They reserved for our group a domed house. The area was overgrown with head-high weeds. We had to cut off thick bushes before we could get into the house. It was still dark. The warden told us to make quick preparations for a resting place in order to sleep till morning.

Nobody among us was able to know exactly where

we were. We only knew this was an old camp abandoned by the former government long time ago. In a state of perplexity, we fell asleep from exhaustion.

The warden did not come until 9:00 a.m. Nobody could sleep well, even though we were tired. We got up early to observe the surroundings and talk with other groups. Finally, we came to know exactly the place where we were. This is Long Giao, city of Long Khanh, on the way to Vung Tau. The camp formerly used by the American troops, was called "Black Horse". We wondered how they could use this place as a reeducation camp because it was devoid of everything.

Repeated orders from the cadres were: take care of the place so that you can sleep and cook! Clean up the surroundings and prepare lunch! With the idea of going camping, we encouraged one another to work hard. As a result, everything was shaping up rather fast and cadres seemed satisfied. At that time, one of our friends let us know that there was an abandoned house filled with ammunition wooden boxes. We then asked the cadres for permission to go get those boxes for pieces of dry wood to sleep on. Luckily, they agreed. We had nothing to eat till 3:00 p.m. that day. Our first meal in the camp was a bowl of rice, some dried fish and vegetable soup. Such a meager meal could not appease our hunger. How do they spend the money we have deposited, I thought. Why do I have to suffer from shortage of food like this? They said we would be served by a restaurant. But it was only hearsay, or just a mere guess. Living with the communists for 13 years, I come to know that nothing is true in what they say. To them, truth does not exist. Back home, after my release in 1988, one of my friends asked me: "What have you learned from the communists?" "Only one thing," I answered, "That is how to lie." I was serious about what I was saying. But my friend could not help bursting into laughter.

That evening, while waiting for dinner, which came very late at 8 o'clock, and while the cadres were absent, a number of Catholic friends and I, we ventured out far from our house and formed a circle to celebrate the Holy Mass together. That was the first Mass we had in camp. The liturgy was simple but really meaningful. We pledged to carry our cross and follow Jesus. We received the Communion, asking Jesus to be our strength while away from home, empty-handed. We offered our own self and our future as an ultimate sacrifice to Him.

My colleagues and I kept gathering in groups very regularly to concelebrate Mass. We had to do it in secret, and with God's help, we were able to do it successfully throughout the period of reeducation. The feeling of being guided and protected by God's love and his providence is a wonderful experience, a miracle, I would say, only known to those who have been in our circumstance. I will have the opportunity to share it in the following chapters.

For about a month, we did nothing special, except sometimes to go deep into the jungle in search of wood for cooking. Time and again, the warden led us to various areas for a clean-up. I began to realize the need of a pair of wooden shoes to walk around with, especially when I was indoors or after a bath. Following others' example, I tried to make a pair of shoes out of the wood of a rubber tree. We used strips of torn cloth as fastening straps nailed down to the shoes by means of barbed wires. This way of shoe-making happened to become big business. But as an old saying goes: "One often dies of one's own career", a former lieutenant commander was busy cutting off barbed wires when a barb flew into the pupil of one of his eyes. He was bleeding terribly. Everybody rushed to help. Some physicians present advised him to take antibiotic to prevent infection. They only put a bandage over his eye for lack of medicine. I asked one of my friends for Tetracycline. My friend did not hesitate to give it to him. Later on, I came to know that his injured eye was almost lost.

During one month's stay at Long Giao, they did nothing to reeducate us. We broke into small groups and followed the wardens to surrounding wastelands. A lot was designated to each group in order to grow manioc and corn. We began to doubt the reeducation time they had promised us. But the job of reeducation required a lot of time, we thought. So, we tried to calm down and encourage one another to be patient. Still, unanswered questions remained in our minds.

As for me, one thing I worried about most was where to find bread and wine for daily Mass. I had brought with me enough supply of bread and wine just for one month, and had used them unsparingly. Now I began to worry. God is everywhere, I know. He resides right in our heart. We can pray to Him anywhere, anytime. But, without celebrating Mass, I, as a priest, cannot offer myself to Jesus as a sacrifice and be in communion with Him to bring down divine grace upon my brothers and sisters, and therefore I feel something missing. I shared that feeling with some of my colleagues. Together, we prayed for God's providence in that very particular moment.

A Religious Soldier

One day, after 6 o'clock dinner, a former captain in a nearby barrack, cut through the fence and came over to see me. "Father, he said, a cadre wants to receive the sacrament of reconciliation. Can you help him?" Very surprised, I answered: "O.K." We thought of a plan to help the cadre. I made an appointment with him in a manioc plantation on Saturday afternoon. I did not forget to tell some of my friends to watch around during our meeting.

That afternoon, keeping my appointment, I stole into the manioc plantation and waited and waited but the cadre did not show up. A few days later, I came to know that he was suddenly put on a special duty, that afternoon. I met him later, and knew he was from Bui Chu. I thought to myself, why not tell him to go to a nearby parish of refugees to inform the pastor of the presence of priests in camp and also ask him for some altar bread and wine. The God-sent cadre had scrupulously complied with all of my requests. During the night, he handed the captain a bottle of altar wine and bread. The captain again cut through the fence to bring those precious gifts to me. I distributed bread and wine to other fellow priests, telling them to use sparingly. I myself used only a drop of wine for each Mass. As a result, the supply of bread and wine lasted for 13 years until the day I was released.

How wonderful God's providence is for his children!

While working in the fields, we had a chance to meet and exchange ideas, thus understanding our mutual needs better. I began to realize the real necessity of priests among others to support their spirit. On Sundays or Saturday afternoons, whenever it was safe, I stole through the fence into a nearby barrack to say Mass for my brothers right at a well. I also went in secret to other areas even to barracks near a stadium where former generals and colonels were detained to visit them. In spite of risk, everybody felt very happy when we met.

Meeting with Rev. Bản

One day, we were sharing dinner when former captain H. ripped through the fence to inform me that Rev. Bản (former chaplain of Cong Hoa hospital) was seriously ill, and he wanted to see me badly. I then told a friend of mine to go get my portion of food for me, and secretly followed the captain to see father Ban. Due to a poor diet in the camp at that time, his health condition was getting worse. After having met him and given some help, I promised to do my best to get him more medicine.

The following day, learning he had been transferred to an infirmary, some of my friends and I tried every means available to bring medicine to him. Thank God! After about a week, he was able to come back and live with his group as usual.

A Heart-rending Encounter

As the camp situation required, we had to get rocks and broken bricks to pave the walkway from the camp-gate.

When people learned that some of our groups often went out of camp to grow corn and manioc, they dressed in disguise, loitering around, hopefully to meet their own folks.

Luckily, the chance had come to one of my friends. One day, he was doing some repair work on the camp-gate with others when a boy about seven recognized his daddy. At his father's sight, the boy rushed to embrace him. A warden present pointed his gun to the sky and fired as a threatening signal to scare the boy away. Out of fear, the boy hugged his daddy even harder. The warden then came to rip the boy away. The suffering father was left in a state of daze while his tearful child was being force-fully pulled out of his arms. Before such a heart-wrenching sight, we became speechless. A heavy silence reigned over us all. Personally, I could never erase that painful picture out of my mind. How sorrowful the poor boy and his mother might be, and how bitterly disappointed the father became at such a terrible situation. I could not get to sleep that night. I tossed around and around restlessly, think-ing of that poor family. I prayed for the mother and her child. I also wanted to console the father. But it was only a mere wish, because he was in a barrack far from mine. I did not forget to pray for him so that he had enough courage to cope with the most painful moment of his life, to survive the ordeal and finally to join his family.Since the day I was re-leased, I have never met him although I still want to know about his fate and his family.

A Propaganda Movie

At that time, there seemed to be much change in the camp. During weekdays, reeducation sessions were sometimes held in the evening. On Sundays and Holidays, we were allowed to play football and volleyball.

One Saturday, we were having lunch when the warden came, giving a piece of information: "You will go to the stadium to see a movie tonight." No-body seemed to be interested in the news. We whispered to one another: "It must be a propaganda movie for sure."

We had dinner as usual, and together, we went to the movie at seven. It was then not quite dark. Some drain-drops began to fall. We asked the warden: "Is attendance optional, sir?" He answered: "All of you must go. It's mandatory. You need a little bit of civilization and culture. The rain is going to let up. Take a piece of nylon along for shelter!" We formed in line and hurried to the stadium. When I got there, I was puzzled to see so many people already there, sitting in front of us. They were all kinds of people belonging to the former regime of the South, including ministers, generals, congressmen, members of various political parties and all religions: Catholics, Buddhists, Protestants, Cao Dai, Hoa Hao followers... They were of different social status then grouped under the same denomination: "Prisoners"

Sitting at the last row, I had the chance to stand up again and again to watch such a rare crowd. I was moved to tears, thinking that a whole regime was driven to this stadium to see a cheap propaganda movie of the Communists. It was about Nguyen Van Troi's story, a so-called hero who had placed a bomb under Cong Ly Bridge in an attempt to murder Mc Namara. I did not even know when the show had started. Never had I felt so humiliated. It was the humiliation of those who had no more homeland, who lost the war without even fighting, whose human rights were explicitly violated and who then were forced to sit on bare ground, under the rain to see a movie of no value at all.

After "Nguyen Van Troi", the show continued with some other cheap propaganda movies. Nobody cared to watch. We took that opportunity to talk and contact one another. The show ended at 11:00 p.m. Group by group, we groped back to camp, feeling deeply humiliated. Man is really "lupus" to man, I thought. I could not bring myself to sleep that night. I began to be in a mental crisis since that day.

Reeducation lessons

Since August, we did not have to labor outside the camp any more. They began to set a reeducation program for us. Some rejoiced, but others worried. We rejoiced at the prospect of being released soon, but we worried, thinking that many months had passed and the release-date was never mentioned. Who could guarantee our release even when the reeducation program was over! Uncertainties were abounding. "To lie like *Vẹm*" as people often say (VEM is an abbreviation for <u>Vie</u>t <u>M</u>inh) haunted our mind. A Southern cadre regrouped in the North had advised us: "When a warden tells you to work hard and compete to get above-norm achievements for the revolution, don't listen to him! You just work as your health condition permits. The reeducation road is still long." We were afraid his prediction would become a reality. Later at camp Tran Phu,

Hoang Lien Son in the North, we also heard a similar advice from a compassionate cadre. That all kinds of possibilities might happen, caused us more anxieties.

Reeducation classes were held in different conference rooms. We were told instructors might come from the central government. There were two classes a day, not including night-workshops and sessions of self-criticism for each barrack. There were ten lectures altogether, focusing on Marxism, proletarian revolution, class-struggle, socialism... These ideals are super, they said. Our revolutionary army is invincible, defeating three predominant imperialist countries such as France, Japan and the United states. Under the humane regime of our government and the guidance of the Party, people will enjoy freedom of religion, abundance of food and the best kind of civilization and culture. Learning the lessons by heart, they talked on and on, shamelessly boasting of imaginary victories. In many instances, there was no truth in what they said. We could not help laughing in secret as a sign of derision. Yes, we pretended to clap our hands to please them.

Once outside the classroom, we kept a world of our own, privately exchanging feelings and thoughts mostly in expression of ridicule and contempt. Many of our friends have recorded in their memoirs quite a few funny stories, ridiculing the foolish simplicity and the incredible ignorance of the Communists. They are like a frog at the bottom of a well, wishing to grow as big as a cow by swelling his belly to the point it breaks. Thinking everybody is ignorant like them, they feel free to say whatever they like. Following is a symbolic anecdote:

A Communist cadre said that the Republic of South Vietnam had spent so much energy and money drilling oil with "Rose" and "Lotus flower" projects. In Thai Binh City up North, under the socialist regime, people just sharpened a bamboo stick, drove it into the ground and oil spurted out in profusion for them to use indefinitely.

Such a miracle of oil is only known to the Communists! Hearing that kind of fake, we could not help laughing. Excuse me, dear Communist friends, when it comes to lying, you're number one and the sky's the limit!

During break-time between two afternoon sessions, a friend came to me, asking for opinion: "How do you think, Father, about the lecture on freedom of religion today?" Reluctant to express my true feelings, I just said: "Let's wait and see!" Hearing that, my friend did not say anything more. Of course, with their three-no-policy (no God, no family, no country) how can they yield to religion. Later when I met my friend in 1979 at camp Ba Sao, Nam Ha, I found that he had thoroughly understood what the Communists really meant when they talked about freedom of religion.

The more they tried to educate us, the better we realize the ignorance of naive cadres, particularly their art of lying. Briefly speaking, everybody found their deceitful nature disgusting. It was rumored that some among young captains unable to stand the Communist oppression had escaped.

Showing off strength

One Sunday, at noontime, all of us were ordered to stay in. Nobody was allowed to go out. The camp atmosphere became very tense.A moment later, Communist troops, armed to their teeth, arrived. They were stationed at different places around the camp while 5 or 7 armored tanks cruised around with cannons and machine-guns pointing to where we were. We had the feeling they were going to fire at us. We are only prisoners or "reeducation students" as they call us, with nothing in hand. How can we do harm to them? What do they fear about us? Or, we thought, they want to show off their strength in retaliation for the shame we have brought to the cadres lately when we often dare to argue with the instructors and their propaganda, proving our knowledge is far superior above theirs. Seemingly, they implied to let us know that army strength talked. Later on, when everything came back to normal, we asked a warden and surprisingly got this answer: "The government wants you all to be protected. Our troops have to sacrifice a lot for your safety." What an answer! Those tactful words were often heard in other camps, too.

It was already Nov. 1975, and still, reeducation

time seemed to drag on indefinitely, which made us both tired and bored. Our future was getting dimmer and dimmer. The cadres turned more and more severe and we became more and more impassive. As for me, I had the feeling of being cheated and trapped tight with no exit. Some of my friends would like to place trust in me. They even discussed with me about their plan of escape. I am a priest, they said, who knows many priests and parishioners in Ho Nai. If we are able to get there, we will certainly be welcome and kept in safety. I could not get to sleep, many nights, restlessly thinking about my current situation. Never had I felt so miserable in my life. As my faith was waning, I sometimes became doubtful of God's providence. I regretted having decided to stay and not to go as my cousin had advised. Now that I lost everything with no solution whatsoever. Although in such a state of mind, every day I tried to keep calm and carry out usual activities with my friends. In the evening, I did not forget to celebrate Mass in secret and say the Rosary with others. While filled with despair, I suddenly got the idea of practicing the Novena (nine-day ritual of prayers) in honor of the Mother of Perpetual Help to ask for spiritual strength, guidance and consolation. On the 6th day of the Novena, it occurred to me that I had to stay in camp for the love of God and for the sake of my friends, too. Like Jesus, I want to become a good shepherd who knows how to sacrifice his own life for his sheep. Do I deserve to be called a priest when I refuse a shepherd's responsibility? With those ideas in mind, I said to myself: "I'd rather die in prison." I, then saw a light at the end of the tunnel, and peace came back to my mind. Life became meaningful to me, again. My new decision turned out to be a source of strength for all my activities during the entire 13 years in prison. It was indeed a special grace from God.

Oh Lord! Thank you for accepting me to die with you on the cross on top of the Calvary for the atonement of my sins and for the salvation of human kind and especially for my friends who are living with me in prison...

Having learned ten lessons of reeducation, we were ordered to move. Some thought we might go home. For me, I felt indifferent. It's good, I thought, if I can go home, if not, it's still O.K with me because I want to share the same fate with my friends.

We were kept in the dark till the end of November 1975 when we found ourselves at Camp Suoi Mau (Spring of blood)

III. CAMP SUOI MAU (SPRING OF BLOOD)

We left Long Giao since dusk and did not arrive
at Camp Suoi Mau until the moon was high above.
We recognized the new place immediately. The
former government of the South had used this camp
to detain Communist prisoners. Buildings in the
camp were of corrugated iron roofs and cement floors.
At the corner remained a chapel and a small pagoda, vestiges of religious freedom. There were different rooms for prisoners to cook and eat and other
rooms for various activities. The camp was surrounded with barbed wires and B40 preventing nets.
Barbed wires were also installed between rows of
barracks to prevent communication. Camp Suoi Mau
was rather small, compared to Long Giao. They
jammed sixty or seventy of us into a barrack. We
had to use a ruler to measure our resting area, about

half size of a mat, for each person. While we were sleeping, a slight move could hit others. We often said jokingly: "We are enjoying the system of 'Canned fish' from the regime."

The next morning, everybody got up, one after the other. The first problem we encountered was how to find water for toilet, or to say jokingly, how to visit Uncle Ho. There were only two sinkholes for the entire camp. We, mostly majors, must wait in a long line. Everybody looked so dumb, so pitiful.

At 9:00 a.m., following the warden's order, we gathered to clean up the campgrounds. The first thing we requested was more rest rooms. Finding it reasonable, he allowed us to start the job. I was among the assigned. We agreed to dig a single row of sinkholes for convenience, although we knew for sure that so many holes close together would cause much more offensive odor. The way sinkholes were made (the way indicated by the revolution) was rather simple and easy. Later, when moving to the North, we knew that those holes were of the same type, everywhere. Some left open, others half-closed, they all served to provide fertilizer for agriculture. The result was that everybody in the North must be familiar with this terrible kind of odor.

During a visit to Hanoi in Jan, 1988, I was greeted by this offensive odor around Lake Hoan Kiem, except around Ho's mausoleum and in areas where foreigners lived. For lack of public restrooms, people often relieved themselves by dropping their body waste anywhere, at the foot of a tree, even on public lawns. Yes, we did see some rare public restrooms, but they were roughly designed the revolutionary way, unable to eliminate such strong odor.

After digging a trench, 60m long, 60cm wide and about 1m deep, we divided it into sections and put logs or pieces of wood on them for a seat. After that, we ran wooden posts along the trench to support sheets of corrugated iron used as roofs and walls around the place. Having got the job done, everybody felt satisfied. Cadres were happy, too. It was well done, indeed. But designed the revolutionary way, it only produced obnoxious results.   Consequently, during the whole time we lived at Suoi Mau, we had to live permanently with the bad smelling coming from those fetid sinkholes, and with flies, too. Flies were everywhere. Never in my life have I seen so many of them.. The whole length of the 4m high fence of barbed wires, East of the camp, was thick with flies, so thick that we could not see through. Due to lack of food, limitation of water and poor sanitation, some of us suffered from severe dysentery producing blood and mucus.

After the job of making sinkholes was finished, some of us followed the warden out of camp in search of wood and abandoned corrugated iron. Therefore, we had a chance to witness the atheists' lifestyles.

Before 1975, most prisons had worship places for religious service, especially for Buddhists and Catholics. As I had mentioned before, at Camp Suoi

Mau, there were a Catholic chapel and a small pagoda facing each other. When passing by the pagoda, I found it empty. But when I turned my eyes toward the chapel, I saw through an open door, a half-naked cadre in shorts sawing a piece of wood in two. Looking further inside, I saw a crucifix still on the altar, but the floor was strewn with wood chips and all kinds of kitchen utensils. Indeed, the chapel had turn into a storehouse. (After being released in 1988, I also found that my chapel at Truyen Tin camp, near the general Staff had become a car garage filled with disabled cars and auto parts. Before such a pitiful sight, I hurried away in disbelief). The Communists do not hesitate to treat sacred places disrespectfully. No wonder they are atheists.

They had no special program for us at Camp Suoi Mau. Day in day out, having nothing to do, we just ate, slept and waited.

To kill time, I learned how to play chess with father NVT, my friend. Many others practiced necromancy (the magic ritual of conjuring up a dead person's soul.) I also tried once, with no result. The reason is because I am a priest, they said. I felt sorry for my friends. During such a difficult time, they tried to do anything, even to resort to necromancy for consolation. From then on, my colleague and I, we sought ways to support our friends spiritually. We celebrated daily Mass in secret for catholic friends and held a private talk with them as a kind of spiritual retreat. We also helped those who wanted to join our faith. The first two friends to be baptized were Mr. Bao and Mr. Phu. What we did in secret, produced good results.

One day, a friend in our barrack shouted painfully from a bout of severe stomachache. Some of former physicians came. The diagnosis was appendicitis. It was an emergency case. It could become fatal if not treated immediately. It was almost sunset. We let the warden know in the nick of time. He was then carried to an infirmary on the other side of the fence. About ten minutes later, we heard a deafening cry of pain from the infirmary. One of my friends said in an affirmative voice: "Surgery is certainly being performed without anesthetic. I don't know if he can survive." As for me, I prayed to the Mother of Perpetual help for him. I knew he was a devout Catholic, a religious major who often attended the Mass I celebrated in privacy and said the Rosary daily.

Miraculously, he survived the surgery. After only a week, when our friend came back to his barrack, he said: "It was so terrifying, my brothers! They did operate on me without anesthetic, and Thank God, I have survived."

Spiritual Activities

It was getting colder and colder at Suoi Mau. Our mood was badly affected by the gloomy weather, too. (When we are sad, how can surroundings ever be bright!) December was already here, reminding us that Christmas was around the corner. As usual, I tried to help our friends prepare their souls for the Advent. Other priests and I, each of us was in charge of a small group, providing spiritual help to those in need. I preached the Gospel and encouraged Catholic friends to get prepared for the sacrament of reconciliation. I also succeeded in helping a number of people in trouble. When we were only two, we walked side by side, talking to each other. If the number of persons was 5 or 6, they walked in two lines, face-to-face, with me in between, preaching to them. Sometimes, we sat in a circle, sharing the words of God. To say the truth, all of us were very devout. We deeply felt the presence of the Holy Spirit in our souls. We pledged to firmly keep our faith, to proclaim the good news of God whenever possible, and to say the Rosary everyday. I strongly felt the spirit of my Congregation (of the Redemptorists) growing in me, which made me happy and enthusiastic to serve my friends, all the more.

On the week before Christmas, we got very excited and thrilled. We dared to ask for permission to celebrate Christmas in public. But we just got an uncertain answer from the warden. The matter is still under consideration, he said. We continued to ask, but as for me, I knew deep inside that as atheists, with their policy of destroying religions, especially Catholicism, they could never grant us such a privilege. Once accepting to die in prison, I had nothing to fear. Thinking so, I continued to make necessary preparations in silence for Christmas.

Jesus to travel by air

Not far from where I lived, beyond a fence of barbed wires was an area reserved for intelligence, military police and military security of the former government. I happened to see my younger brother (D.N.T) there. We were so happy to meet. Reporting for reeducation after me, my brother might be better supplied than I. Therefore he expressed an intention to throw over the fence to me some of his warm clothes. But I refused, thinking that he might need those things more than I did. My brother let me know that there were no priests in his barrack, that people over there were also anxious to celebrate Christmas. I then wrote a few lines on a piece of paper, crumpled it into a ball and threw it over the fence, informing them of the date and time when I could hear their public confession. I had to do so many times before Christmas.

How about the Communion? This liturgy was harder to realize. I must carefully select a trustworthy person, willing to serve as a Eucharistic minister, and he must be in permanent contact with me. Luckily, I found a right man to do the job. He was a former police officer.

We agreed to meet on Christmas' eve. On that day, the Communists were put on the alert. As the staff did not want us to have Christmas, they kept armed guards around the camp all day to watch over us. We found it very difficult to execute our plan. We tried our best, however, for the love of God. We waited till lunch time when very few cadres were around. At the sight of an armed guard, some of us went out to greet him right in front of the barrack, talking with him on and on, trying to divert his attention while I with some others hurried to the fence with the Eucharist. At my signal, the Eucharistic minister appeared on the other side of the fence, ready. I then flew the Eucharist to him.

After Christmas, I was informed that many had received the Holy Communion that night. Each piece of bread had been broken in four to fill the need. Later, Jesus must "travel by air" like that many times.

The Holy Night of 1975:
The First Christmas in prison.

As Christmas Day drew near, Church bells in Ho Nai area chimed resoundingly to greet the coming of Jesus Christ, which made us homesick. Never did I become as homesick as on that emotional moment. Many of us could not help weeping. I was not able to hold my tears, either.

Memories rushed back to me. I was then a chief chaplain for the special military zone of the Capital. During Christmas season, my duty was to find enough priests (usually 22, 23) for various military units under my control to fulfill pastoral ministries such as celebrating Mass, hearing confessions, delivering sermons... Some units were far away, as far as Con Son Island. Preparations had to be made 4 or 5 months in advance. Personally, I had to celebrate evening Mass, midnight Mass and morning Mass in main areas. Now that I am detained here as a prisoner, I thought to myself and felt so miserable.

Anyway, we decided to celebrate Christmas Mass for our friends, even without permission. Once we had been used to doing things in secret, there was nothing for us to fear. No pompous external ceremonies, of course. They were not necessary for internal fervor. As for music, we had all kinds of Christmas songs echoing day and night from the loudspeakers in nearby parishes. There were six priests in our place. On Christmas' eve, each priest was in charge of one group. They secretly celebrated Mass whenever and wherever available: behind a kitchen, a broken ox-cart or at a building corner. God chose to be born into this world in a humble place exactly as he had been born two thousand years ago. I was the latest to celebrate midnight Mass, at the request of the majority. My group was rather large, with at least 70 participants, a combination of Catholics, Protestants, Buddhists (the story of a Buddhist attending that night Mass will be detailed, later, and I can never forget to thank God for such a precious gift.) The Mass took place in the open air, on the cement ground, near a sinkhole. That's the most suitable place we could find. I dressed better to suit the occasion, with a pair of wooden shoes made at Long Giao, in patchy shorts and a used shirt supplied by the camp. My hair was well-combed. (To prove that I am a well-behaved person, my hair was always kept glossy during my stay in camp.) No sooner had we arrived at the gathering place than an armed guard passed by. We pretended as if nothing were going to happen. We said "hello" to him before he left. We then started our first Christmas Mass in prison. I crossed myself, wished peace to my friends and shared with them some words of God. At that emotional moment, everybody cried.

The Mass lasted for only 5 minutes, but full of meanings. The Catholics received the Communion, asking Jesus to keep company with them always and to be present in their lives during the difficult time. The non-Catholics came with a sincere heart, asking for more courage to face all the trials of life. After the Mass, everyone went in peace, safe and sound.

That night, I was invited to a Christmas party organized by a small group. We had tea and plain rice-soup served with sugar. Some other groups might be supplied with better food and drink.

Major Ngac's Poem
Respectfully to Rev. Que
I always remember the day when
The altar left in the dark,
The manger at a sinkhole,
You and I, father, we prayed in whispers:
"Glory to God in the Highest,

And peace to people on earth."
How sublime! How serene!
I, a pagan, overwhelmed with emotion;
You looked so beautiful, that night!
More beautiful than ever!
With no black cassock,
No white collar,
Yet, you radiated the aura of a God's child.
How sublime you were!

This is to remember Rev. Dinh Ngoc Que at Camp
Suoi Mau, on Christmas, 1975.
With best whishes to:
Rev. Dinh Ngoc Que
Rev. Phan Phat Huon
Rev. Ngo Dinh Thoa
Rev. Nguyen Van Trung
And all other friends

Christmas' 75
Nguyen Dinh Ngac

My first Christmas in prison at Camp Suoi Mau
in 1975 brought more results that I had expected.
Early in 1988, I was set free and came back to
Saigon after 13 years of reeducation in various camps.
One day, at around 4 o'clock in the afternoon, when
I stayed at 38 Ky Dong St., the reception bell rang.
After that, the door-keeper came to let me know
someone wanted to see me. I opened the door, and,

105

to my surprise, saw Major Ngac. He was the one who had worked with me in the psychological warfare Bureau at the Special Military Zone of the Capital before 1975. He had also attended the midnight mass I celebrated at Camp Suoi Mau.

Now we met again, after long years of separation. What a wonderful surprise! He proudly said to me: "Father, I come here today to see you, and particularly to bring you good news. I have decided to become a Catholic. Since the night with you at the first Christmas in prison, I was deeply impressed by your courage, your strong faith-life and constantly kept an inquiring mind ever since. Especially while reading the New Testament Book published by the Catholic chaplain Directorate,I found "La Raison d'être", a strange attraction and a source of strength to meet all the challenges of my prison life. Therefore, back home from prison, I expressed my intention to become a Catholic to my wife and family. Everyone welcome my decision. Please, help me if you can, father." I accepted his request with much respect and admiration.

Three months later, he informed me of his departure to the U.S. with his family. He was allowed to go, thanks to his H.O. status. I was happy at the news, but regretted not being able to baptize him in time. I advised him to keep his promise with God when in America. He asked me to pray for his safety and his family's. I had given him and his family my blessings before he left.

As a H.O.14 member, I left for the U.S. in 1993. I celebrated the opening Mass for the first time at the Blessed Sacrament Church, Westminster with the participation of a great number of family members and friends. After the Mass, a reception was held in my honor. On that occasion, I again met major Ngac and his family. He came to greet me and let me know he and some of his family members had been baptized right here in this church. I was so happy for him, his wife and children. I thanked God for him and his family.

How mysterious God's love is! Being loved by God is really a big privilege for mankind. Jesus had been born right in major Ngac's heart, a Buddhist of good will, on the First Christmas at Camp Suoi Mau.

Hearing the news of his death in 1995, I came to his funeral, said a Requiem Mass for him and shared God's words with his family members and friends. During the sermon, I testified to his faith and courage. Hearing the story of how he had become a Catholic, people could not hold their tears.A Buddhist, one of his relatives, represented the bereaved family to thank all the priests present and the Catholic Community, saying:" The fact that Mr. Ngac, a high-ranking officer, an intellectual (graduated from law school) has gone through the ups and downs of life and finally became a Catholic, is what we have to admire and follow as a good example."

After Mass, when concelebrants and I went into the sacristy, they said to me: "What you and the bereaved family's representative have said today, will certainly make many more people come to God." In silence, I prayed that what they said would become a reality.

Until now, I still remember Mr. Ngac and his family and always pray for them, hoping the rest of his family will become God's children and share His heritage in Heaven.

Sept. 12, 1997

IV. ADVANCING TO THE NORTH (10-06-1976)

Under Ngo Dinh Diem regime, when the phrase "advancing to the North" was heard, everybody was exhilarated, thinking it was a lofty goal to break off the fetters, to liberate the North from the yoke of Communism and atheism, from starvation, under-development, and from a deteriorating culture. Actually at that time, the South could have easily realized that plan if it had not been prevented by the United States. After April 30, 75, when the country was unified, we came to know the wretched existence of the North and realize that the former government had been right with its idea of liberating the North. Instead of liberating the South, I would say, the North should be liberated first. What has happened is certainly against God's will. No wonder the unification of the country realized by the Com-

munists only makes the South poorer and consequently brings disaster to the whole nation.

What we thought would happen, was inevitable.
News of moving was spreading all over the camp.
Camp activities began early that morning. We were
ordered to get packing. Each one of us was allowed
to take along only 20 kg. All heavy stuffs must be
left behind. Drinking cans, wood or iron objects,
pointed devices... all were stacked in one place.

Some were naive enough to say: "We might gather
at Marine Base Sóng Thần for the end-of-course
ceremony before being released by the clement revolutionary government." All guesses however ended
up in smoke. We waited till evening when Molotovas
arrived in groups. We were then ordered to get
aboard. Each twenty of us must squeeze in one car.
Closely-covered Molotovas were packed with so many
people that they had to sit on one another's knees.
The air inside was getting unbearably stuffy and
oppressive. I perspired all over. I prayed in silence, asking Jesus to help me walk the way of His
cross. After about half an hour, the convoy began to
roll. Looking out through a hole in the canvas, many
of us thought we were on the way to Saigon. Some
were very optimistic. They entertained the idea of
being released soon. The convoy crossed Saigon
Bridge only to turn left into Saigon Newport. Under
the bright lights at the port appeared a number of
freighters ready for us. Where to go, Phu Quoc or
Con Son, we asked ourselves? We heard that some

of our friends had been taken there. Everybody looked anxious. We were ordered to go down and get in line to climb aboard, one after the other. A shaky ladder hung steep against the side of the ship served as the only entrance. My hair stood on end when I watched people risk their lives, trying to climb up the ladder under the pressure of Communist cadres who kept urging them to go fast. I personally saw a person miss a step and fall down to the river. The cadres, however, did not care to rescue him. He must be drowned in the dark, cold water... I could do nothing but pray for him, thinking to myself how cheap human life is to the Communists!

To my estimate, that night, ship "Song Huong" must accommodate at least 1000 people. Our group was the last to climb aboard. I took all the precautions I could and succeeded in getting into the ship. As a freighter, it was so dirty. The ship bottom was divided in several holds. Four hundred of us were jammed in one hold. We could hardly find a place to rest among piles and piles of baggage. We had to sit tight with arms around knees, exactly like canned fish. One of our friends had to hang up a hammock over our heads in order to sleep. The voyage did not start until very late at night. When the roof of the boat began to shut down, we became almost suffocated. Some shouted and yelled angrily. A riot almost broke out before cadres threatened to shoot. They had to give in, finally, allowing the roof to be left open about 2m for the air to come in. Nobody was able to sleep, that night. The ship traveled through Nha Be River into the ocean. We just guessed, but nobody knew where we were going. Only dried food made in China and instant noodle were served in the morning and in the evening. As for drink, a can of water per day was allowed for each person. The purpose was to limit toilet activities. This was the hardest job. At the corner of the hold were placed two barrels covered with two large mats for toilet. Each person was provided with two nylon bags for urination. Yes, we were given means of relieving ourselves. But how to use them was quite a problem. Can you imagine the situation when so many people go to toilet in a narrow hold of the ship, right where they eat and sleep? Adding to the misery was the strong bad smelling of body's waste matter which filled the air throughout a long voyage. Due to a great number of people, two barrels were soon filled. Time and again, we had to carry them up deck in order to dump the putrid waste into the ocean. While moving, the barrels dropped the waste everywhere in the ship, smearing even those sitting and lying around. In addition, the washing and cleaning were very limited for shortage of water, which made the situation even more unbearable.

During a sanitation-round, a former naval officer stood on deck, observing around. The ship is moving Northward, he said in an affirmative voice. As he was a specialist, we all agreed in silence, a heavy silence... We are being deported, alas, thanks to the clemency of the Revolution, I thought to myself. Only God knows how our future will be.

Night was falling again, some of the priests and I gathered in secret for the first Mass on board. A number of Catholics were also present at the Mass. We prayed to God for enough strength to walk the way of the cross with Him to the end, and to empty His bitter cup. Not being able to stand the misery during the voyage, a former lieutenant colonel poisoned himself that night and died before we knew it.

We informed the cadres of the bad news, early in the morning. They had the body carried up deck. Everybody thought it would be dumped into the ocean. On the contrary, it was kept on board till the end of the voyage. That was the first prisoner to be buried in the Northern land. I prayed for him, in particular. He might have chosen another life, which must be much better than this one created by the Communists.

Ha Ly Port, Hai Phong

When the ship arrived at Hạ lý port, the first thing they did was to bury the corpse. We were ordered to get ready for the landing. A cadre dressed in yellow, *"nón cối"* over head, pistol at waist, and loudspeaker in hand, proudly shouted at us: "This is the land of socialism. It is a great honor for you to be here for the first time." With much satisfaction, he kept repeating those words again and again for fear we did not pay enough attention to what he had said. As a person who had been at Ha Ly port in 1950, I did not feel honored at all to be back here, again. The environment was somewhat familiar, yet everything seemed to change for the worse. Nothing appeared new but cracked walls covered with moss and old buildings in ruins all around.

The train was ready for us. We took turns to get aboard. Carriages had only one opening at the back as most of them were used for carrying animals. Forty persons including baggage for each. When a carriage was filled to capacity, the back entrance began to shut down, letting no air in. Later, we heard that someone died right in a carriage from exhaustion and also for lack of air. The aged train (left behind from French colonial time) started to move with difficulty, whistling noisily and spouting up puffs of sky-blackening smoke.

At Camp Suoi Mau, we had to take measurements inch by inch for a small lot to sleep. In Song Huong ship, we had to squat with arms around knees like fish in a can. And now in the land of socialism (as they call it), animal-carriages were used to carry us. Nowhere is human condition worse than in this socialist land, where human beings are treated no better than animals.

We got down the train and were classified as among the lucky.They took us to a store-house, that night. The long-abandoned structure was an iron-frame covered on top and all around with torn sheets of corrugated iron. We roughly cleaned the cement ground for a temporary place to lie down. We were lucky to have a pool of water near the storehouse. We came to know later that it was a bomb hole left behind by the Americans during an air-attack on Hai Phong. Not worrying about the water condition, not even caring to ask permission, we jumped down the pool, trying to wash ourselves and do the laundry to our satisfaction. That night, they distributed dried food early to us so that we could eat and go to sleep. As soon as we lay down, some began to snore; others to talk at random in a bad dream. The later the night, the more shoutings in panic were heard. Most of us were seemingly going through a nightmare. A number of priests and I woke up and celebrated together the first Mass under the cover of dark night in the land of socialism. We thanked God for a safe voyage. We prayed for everybody, ready to say "Fiat" for an uncertain future. We prayed that God would become our shield protecting us, a source of strength for us to cope with the trials of a new prison life. After Mass, I came back to my place and soon fell asleep. When I got up in the morning, some friends asked me:" Last night, we heard you snore and talk at random and sometimes shout in panic. Why?" I really did not know what had happened. I only knew that during the night, I could hardly get to sleep, and while sleeping, I had many nightmares, and when I woke up, I got panicked and perspired all over. I was indeed deeply affected by recent terrible happenings.

They allowed us to rest until about noon-time when we were ordered to gather for injection against diseases. Actually, until now I do not know with what kind of medicine they have injected us. Only to my recollection, do I know that after being injected, we were given a banana for health-improvement as they said.

Late in the afternoon, a train appeared in the distance, moving with difficulty, nearer and nearer. A few minutes later, the whistle started blowing for a long moment before the train stopped right where we were gathering. Again, we climbed up animal carriages just like the day before. My heart sank at the thought of being treated once more like animals. I prayed for a safe journey. The train rolled with great effort across a rice-field. We saw through a hole in the canvas the poor countryside under the dim light of a late afternoon. I had the feeling we were crossing a desert, as the field was not in planting season at that time. I had a chance to see with my own eyes the abject poverty of the Northerners. Once in a while, the train passed by a village with sparse mud-walled,thatch-roofed houses. Population must be thin. A special sight caught our attention. In each village, there was a house with red-tiled roofs used to keep cattle. As you know, cows and buffaloes in a socialist country receive better treatment than human beings because they are treasured for labor.

During a night-long travelling, our living condition in the train was terrible, not fit for human beings. Our misery had no boundaries. Jammed in animal-carriages, we ate, slept and went to toilet at the same place without any kind of sanitation. Luckily, nobody died along the way. That night, I celebrated Mass by myself in secret, praying for spiritual strength and consolation.

The Red River

The train did not stop till noon, the following day, at a by-station by the Red River. We got down and walked about 15 minutes before reaching a ferryboat.

Strangely enough, a number of female cadres and local people had been there with hot green tea for us. They said: "Feel free to drink it." And then added provokingly: "Even though you have sinned against people and the Revolution, you are still well-treated with generosity by the people."

Yes, people may be generous, I thought to myself, as for the Revolution, I am not sure; I have to think again. Let's wait and see. Since the day I reported for reeducation, they have done nothing that makes me happy. They only treat us with rancor, hatred, retaliation, oppression and torture.

After about half an hour of rest, they gave us order to embark on the ferryboat. The boat was rather old, but large enough to accommodate hundreds of people.

Standing on the boat, I looked around, admiring the beauties of nature. The majestic river kept rolling along, carrying with it abundance of rich silt, fertilizing the land wherever it goes. I praised God for his love of my country. Man can be cruel, inhuman, unfaithful, but Mother Vietnam is always benevolent, forgiving with her open arms ready to protect, support and do good to those who come to her with a repentant heart.

It might be the first time I saw the Red River. While crossing it, I felt I had more love for it and for mother Vietnam. After half an hour when we reached the other side of the river, molotovas had been there, waiting for us. We did not know where they were going to take us.

Jungle of Yen Bai

The convoy advanced deep into a jungle known to us later as Yen Bai. We stopped at a clearing where a number of tents had been set up. The cadres said to us: "Here is your designated place. You have to find food and shelter by your own means to support yourselves". At nightfall, we were divided into small groups. One tent was reserved for each group. An only hurricane-lamp in each tent did not give enough light for us. We had to grope our way to a sleeping place. Before sleeping, I did not forget to celebrate in secret the first Mass in the jungle of Yen Bai. I prayed with devotion for everybody. I surrendered my body and soul to God and put my own fate in His hand. His will must be done. I felt the need to put more warm clothes on, as the night was getting cold in the jungle, and thank God, I soon fell into a rather sound sleep.

A narrow Escape from Death, the first time

The warden came at 10:00 the next morning. He gathered us for the division of jobs. The first group was assigned to clear and clean up the surroundings. Another group to look for wood in the jungle for cooking. The last one (including me and Rev. Trung) to carry logs home to build an enclosure in order to hold water for kitchen needs. We went deep into the woods, looking for logs. Finally, we found a dead tree about 30cm in diameter, and 20m in length. We had to muster all strength to carry the tree on our shoulders, weaving it along the foot of a hill. Our trip came to a final stage when one of our friends slipped and fell down. The whole group lost balance and in panic dropped the tree, causing its long foot to hit me right on the head. My head turned around and around before I fell down and rolled over several times on the steep hillside. Everybody including Rev. Trung thought I might have died or at least had been seriously injured. They rushed to my rescue, but saw me only smeared with mud, suffering a minor headache. Thank God, I had miraculously survived the accident.

Since then, I kept worrying the whole week, and whenever I went out for labor, I prepared myself to die and prayed to my guardian angel to protect me and others.

After about 3 months at Yen Bai, as planned, we had to move to camp Tran Phu, near Tran Phu tea plantation. The trip was very arduous, as we were forced to walk more than 10 km before reaching the destination.

V. CAMP TRAN PHU
AND CAMP HOANG LIEN SON 3.

We left Yen Bai for camp Tran Phu and then Hoang Lien Son 3. The more we went, the deeper we got into a miserable life. Nothing new happened. Our lives just changed for the worse. During the first Mass I celebrated in secret at Camp Tran Phu, I prayed for myself and friends, for sufficient strength to face the challenge of a prison life, and for enough courage to show the undaunted spirit of a true nationalist.

At Camp Tran Phu, I was assigned for labor and ranked among the strongest who must work hard to meet the norm. Everyday, I must go up hill and down dale, in search of various kinds of trees and bamboos for building houses: wood trees for house-pillars, bamboos and *Luồng* (of bamboo-family, but larger) for roofs and nửa (another kind of bamboo) for weaving roof-thatch. Everybody was busy working. The job was so arduous, requiring a lot of effort and patience. We had to build not only houses for ourselves (as the cadres often said), but houses for them, too. In addition to main dwellings, we must set up kitchens, dining rooms, meeting halls, culture houses, reception rooms... seemingly to prove that we had everything needed for reeducation.

We toiled and moiled under the hot sun and heavy rain, in sprite of danger, hunger, inclement weather and unhealthy living conditions in the jungle. We did it all for the purpose of being released after three years as they often said. The well-reeducated would have a better chance to return home soon.

Following are lifetime memories:

The winter in 1976 was unusually cold. Some day, the mercury went down to 6° or 7° C, which could kill men and cattle. So far, none of us had died from the cold. No matter how cold it was, we must go to work. The warden said: "You can have a break only when the mercury drops to 5°." Sometimes, we had to dig a pond to raise fish. Sometimes, we had to get down the cold water to collect mud and mix it with shredded straw under our feet to cover walls.

Surviving another brush with death at camp Hoang Lien Son 3

One day, in spite of the cold and slippery weather,

a number of friends and I were assigned to cut trees in the jungle for house-pillars. I came upon a tree of standard size down in the valley, while others were working on the trees overhead. At about noontime, when I was busy chopping the tree, a sudden gust of wind came. The whole forest shook. The strong wind blowing in different directions did not allow us to fell the trees the direction we wanted. The trees, half-cut at the foot, began to fall in all directions, which threatened everybody's life. A tree knocked down by the wind hit another half-cut one, making it fall and roll down the valley to where I was working. Hearing screams of fear from friends overhead, I got panicked and jumped into a near-by hole, just before the tree crashed and lay right across the hole. The crash was so violent that I was shaken all over and fainted. I had fainted for how long I did not even know. I did know that when regaining consciousness, I looked up and saw people around the hole, ready for the rescue. They thought I might have died. But when they saw me open my eyes, they showed happiness and hurried to pull me up. Later, back to camp, they let me know at that time my face was "as pale as a leaf"

During the Mass I celebrated in secret, that night, I offered my thanks to God for having saved my life so that I could continue to serve Him and others through all the tribulations of life. Living in the same boat, we became close friends. We depended on one another for love, encouragement and consolation. After the accident, I was assigned to a group growing vegetables instead of going outside for labor.

An Eight-tree penalty for a Priest because of a substandard one.

The so-called policy of "releasing prisoners after three years of good reeducation" gave birth to a number of people called informers or "antenne" (French word). The Communists usually play one prisoner off against the other, thus turning the prisoners into the wardens' eyes and ears. Informers do not hesitate to achieve something to win a small favor even at the expense of their friends, hopefully to be released sooner.

One day, we were assigned to get *Vầu* (another kind of bamboo) for making roofs. Four trees of the right size was the norm to be reached by each person. In the afternoon, when the leader of my group came to collect the trees, I sincerely said to him: "I've got four trees as assigned, chief. But I would like to let you know that one of them is a little bit smaller. I think it's old and good enough, anyway." He reassured me: "Don't worry, dad, it's O.K." With my mind at peace, I came back to my barrack.

At nightfall, the warden came. He gathered us in one place, gave us a black look and stressed each of his words, saying: "Who of you have not achieved the norm for Vầu, raise your hand." He repeated his request three times. Finally, one hand was raised:

"It's me, sir! I missed one tree." The warden chided him for a while. After that, he said: "Here is penalty for you. This coming Sunday, you must go get another tree in compensation." After a while, he raised his menacing voice again: "There's still another one among you who failed to achieve the norm, I know. Let him be sincere and put up his hand, now. He cannot hide anything from me. He will regret if I have to disclose his name." Everybody felt uneasy and annoyed. Whispers were heard, urging a sincere confession. In perplexity, I thought to myself: "I've got enough trees as requested although one of them is a little bit smaller. The tree, however, has been approved by the leader of my group. Somebody must have overheard and reported it to the warden. What to do now?" After a brief moment of hesitation, I courageously raised my hand, saying: "I've got four trees as requested, but one of them is slightly smaller." Hearing that, the warden showered curses upon me: "You are a dishonest priest, an insincere worshipper of God and Mary. I'm going to let you know the way Revolution will treat this kind of people like you. This Sunday, you must go get 8 full trees in compensation." Deep inside, I felt very much insulted. I wanted to argue. I held my tongue in time and decisively pledged to God: "Oh Lord! I can die for you. But I don't want you, my Lord, to be maligned by these gross atheists. I promise you to get 8 trees to shut them up."

On Sunday, everybody stayed home as usual,

except me and the person who had been fined one tree. With a knife in hand, and an empty stomach, we started early in the morning. We crossed a stream and went about 200m further before climbing to the mountain top for Vầu (I don't know why Vầu only grow on mountain-tops.) With one tree cut down as fined, my friend went back, leaving me alone among the immensity of nature. Again and again, I sang religious songs in Vietnamese, in French even in Latin to soothe myself. After singing, I whistled and whistled, producing sounds echoing in the forest. I had chopped down six trees by noon. Two more needed to be cut. Too tired and hungry (because I did not have breakfast, that morning) I wanted to return to camp for lunch and then came back to work. But I balked at the idea. It was too time-consuming. It occurred to me to look for exotic fruits in the wilderness to appease my hunger.

Just like a miracle!

I went down the mountain and turned to a grove. To my recollection, cadres had told us there were edible fruits growing in the wild. They hung in white bunches on trees like strings of heavy beads around the neck of ladies. When I entered the grove near the valley, I felt refreshed. The air was so invigorating! Looking up, I saw a few trees white with fruit in the distance. At a closer look, they looked like the ones described by the cadres. I put the knife down and climbed up a tree to taste-test some of them. The sweet-smelling flavor and the fructose helped me regain strength. Without hesitation, I ate my fill and still saved a hatfull.

I felt so delighted at that unexpected event, thinking to myself: "It is not a chance-happening. It certainly happens by God's providence. God feeds birds in the sky and fish under the ocean, let alone those who revere and love Him."

I went back to the mountaintop for two more trees to achieve the number requested. After that, I tied each two in a bundle. Together, I had four bundles. When I got the job done, the night fell, as the sun set so fast behind mountains. I had to carry one by one back to camp, since I was not strong enough for four bundles at the same time. I had to report to armed guards each time I arrived at the camp gate. Four trips were to be made from start to finish.

It was almost 8:00 p.m. when I arrived at my barrack. My friends gathered around me for news. One of them said: "The warden and a number of friends have intended to look for you this evening. At your sudden appearance at the gate, the cadre told us: "Leave Que alone! If someone wants to help him, let that person do it by himself. We love you, father, but we don't know what to do." I really appreciated my friends for their sympathetic attitude. Finally, one friend said: "Go get something to eat, Dad! You must be hungry and tired after a day's hard work." I replied: "How can I eat while covered with sweat like this. Let me take a bath first." Such a fraternal love made me forget everything. I went to a nearby stream and waded into the water to wash myself. I felt refreshed and unusually relieved at the idea that I had got the job done as I wished. Thank God for having fed me like a small bird in the jungle. After a quick bath, I felt cold and hurried to put on my dress. On the way back to camp, suddenly my entire body shook with a burning sensation. I felt dizzy and nauseated. My vision became blurred. I hurried to bed where dinner was ready and told a neighbor to help me set the food aside so that I had enough room to sleep. I lay down and covered myself with a blanket. Knowing I had a bad fever, my friends came to help. I had worked hard all day with an empty stomach and then I had taken a cold bath while my body was still covered with sweat. That was the reason of my fever. After drinking hot water and taking some medicine from my friends, I fell into a bad sleep.

Close to Death the Third time

The following morning, when everyone got up for labor as usual, I lay half-awake, unable to get out of bed. One of my friends saw me while doing sanitary work in the building. He then reported my situation to the warden. It was the person who had penalized me for a slightly smaller tree just because I was a priest. I did not know if he regretted having been cruel to me lately or not. His attitude however seemed to soften when he said to my friend: "A doctor will come here soon. Remember to tell him to visit Mr. Que." A moment later, the doctor came. After the diagnosis, he took my temperature. It was 41° C. He gave me a dose of black pills, trying to bring my temperature down, but in vain. It was a kind of Oriental Medicine fabricated by the Army, I thought. The fever did not abate. I continued to take a dose twice a day, and have only liquid soup. My temperature stayed the same for several days. Many feared I would not be able to survive that time. A friend went over a nearby barrack and got me two pills of Pharmaton. I took one pill a day without the warden knowing. Luckily, after two days, my temperature fell to 38°. (Actually Pharmaton is only a kind of tonic. In my case, however, it turns out to be effective. I just don't understand why.)

I took Quinacrine for two more days before the fever stopped.

I had been seriously ill after so many days of hard work in the jungle without adequate food. And now just one day after being recovered from fever, I was forced to go out for labor again. I did not want to ask permission to stay home. I tried to go with my friends. In sympathy, they took turns to help me achieve the norm set for that day: to get a bundle of *nứa* (another kind of bamboo) and smash them for weaving roof-thatch.

Sitting at the foot of a tree in the depth of the jungle, I was moved to tears while watching friends enthusiastically chop down the trees for themselves and also for me. Such an overflowing show of brotherly love made me both sad and happy at the same time. I felt deeply sorry for all of us being treated as prisoners. My eyes blurred with tears, I prayed to God for an early deliverance, asking Him for more physical and spiritual strength to overcome all trials of life so that we could meet our dear ones, some day.

From the bottom of my heart, I offer my thanks to God and to those who have saved my life and helped me through the difficult times. Until now, I still remember what they have done for me and pray for them always.

Since the day I was recovered from a bout of fever, my health and physical endurance subsided very fast. Each time I went out for labor, I felt extremely bored and depressed...

The Power of Truth

The camp where I lived was about 12 km from Inter-camp 2. In addition to usual work done to sustain ourselves daily such as growing potato, manioc, corn, rice..., sometimes we had to go to Inter-camp 2 for the necessities of life: rice, dried manioc, dried potato, *bobo* (sorghum), salt, fish sauce, sugar, lard. We went, light-handed but on the way back, each one of us had to carry at least 12kg. We started early, but did not reach home till late in the evening.

As mentioned above, I had to carry on my shoulders 12kg of rice. I tied up two bottom-parts of the pants, filled them with rice and then fastened the upper part tight with a belt. With the load around my neck, I started for the camp. I had to stop many times to rest on the way because the rice was heavy. While I was crossing a stream, for some reason, a cadre called me, but I did not know why I could not hear him. It might be that I was too tired or because of the babbling sound of the stream. It was a home-front cadre wearing "*nón-cối*" and with a pistol at his waist. He rushed to me from behind and shouted angrily: "Mr Que! I'm calling you. Why don't you answer me? You dare to despise me. Don't you know that I have the right to discipline you? As a priest, you used to be given the privilege of an easy, idle life of those born with a silver spoon in their mouth. You used to lull people into inactivity and teach them superstitions. You cannot do so now with the Revolution. If you despise me, I don't let you go unpunished." He kept showering curses upon me. What he said was quite irrelevant, bearing no relation whatsoever with my conduct. It did not make sense to me either. With a polite attitude, I replied: "I really did not hear you, sir. How could I hear you while I was too tired and you called me from far behind. If I had heard you, I would certainly have answered you, especially you are a cadre." Not satisfied with my sincere explanations, he emphasized each of his threatening words: "If you

131

scorn me, I'll let you know what stuff I'm made of." I really did not understand what he meant by saying so. I tried to walk far from him, thinking why the Communists bear so much animosity against the priests.

It was twilight when I arrived at the camp. The home-front cadre ordered me to wait in the kitchen yard. I stopped there alone, waiting as all others stepped into barracks. Luckily, the camp head happened to pass by. Seeing me, he asked: "Why do you stand here?" I reported to him the problem between me and the home-front cadre. Hearing the story, the camp-head was seemingly not quite satisfied with the way the home-front cadre had treated me. He then said to me: "Take rice to the kitchen and go back to barrack! Let me solve this problem." I felt somewhat relieved, thinking if something happened, the head would interfere.

Back to camp, I still felt uneasy, not sure about the consequences. That night before bed-time, when I let the mosquito-net fall, one colleague stole into my bed. In secret we concelebrated Mass to thank God for what we had been through. I offered Him all my worries and anxieties, praying for His enlightenment and wisdom to face the trials and evils caused to us by those who are against religion.

The following evening, when I came home after a day of hard work, the warden called me to his office, telling me to write a review of what had happened between me and the home-front cadre, the day before. I came back to barrack and finished my paper in half an hour. With the knowledge that the home-front cadre had told the warden to force me to admit having despised him, I determined to stand firm on my ground at any cost. I had to write the review-paper five times, and not any of those times, did I admit my guilt. I just wrote those five papers in different ways to convey the same truth: the sin of despising the cadre is not mine. Or to put it more clearly, I wanted to tell the truth by cleverly insinuating that the home-front cadre himself was guilty, not me.

One day, after work, the warden called me again to his office. He spoke to me with menace in his voice: "If you keep refusing to admit your sin, you shall be punished." After that, he told me to go back to re-write the review paper. Back to camp, I became more resolute to stand my ground. I began to write the review again, saying the same truth: I am innocent.

After submitting the paper, I waited for the whole week, but nothing happened. A few days later, the warden sent for me. That time, the atmosphere was totally different. He received me with open arms. He invited me to sit on a chair and treated me to a cup of tea and cigarette. I refused to smoke, and reached out for the cup of tea, but did not drink it. He said to me with a smile: "Brother Que, we haven't talked confidentially for a long time, have we? Today, I just want you to know that you're an honest and hard worker. As for the problem you've had with the home-front cadre, I advise you to admit your fault once and for all. What do you think?" Thinking for a short moment, I answered: "Thank you for your concern, sir. But let me tell you the truth. He called me, but I didn't hear him. That doesn't mean I despise him. As a priest, I always teach people the truth and live by the truth. If I am not truthful, I do not deserve being called "priest". Therefore I never tell a lie in my life. Actually, I did not despise the cadre. I did not answer him just because I did not hear him. That's all. I thank you for being kind enough to care about me, but you know, I cannot admit the sin I have not committed. Please, do not force me!" Upon those sincere words of mine, his attitude changed suddenly. His face got pale. He pounded his fist on the table, saying angrily: "I have tried to resolve this matter for you, but you don't listen to me. Stubborn as you are, you have to suffer the consequences." After that, he sent me away.

Back to the building, after telling the news to some of my friends, I packed up shorts, underwears, one drinking can, one rice-bowl and a pair of chopsticks, ready for disciplinary measures. To me, the Mass I celebrated in privacy that night seemed to be at the garden of Gethsemane on the Mount of Olives: "Father, if it is possible, let this chalice pass from me. Nevertheless not as I will, but as thou will." *(St. Matthew XXVI, 39)*

I could not get to sleep all night. I have accepted to die in prison, I thought to myself, now I am ready to die for the sake of truth.

The following day, I went out with others for labor as usual. I was always obsessed with the idea of being disciplined; but strangely enough, one week and then one month passed without anything happening to me, although I met the warden every day. If they want to discipline me, I guessed, they must get the camp-head's approval first. But how can the camp head agree with them whereas they are so unreasonable? So, they just let my case sink down. I was thankful to God and to the Virgin Mary for the strength of truth. God is truth, the eternal truth. To Him, falsehood must be eliminated.

A Senior's Statement
(At Camp Hoang Lien Son 3)

On the way to Inter-camp 2 for food, we usually passed by a hamlet at *Nghĩa Lộ*. Armed guards often allowed us to stop there for rest. By observation, we knew that they were very much interested in the young girls there. As soon as we stopped, they disappeared quickly, leaving us alone. During their absence, curious villagers often came out to talk with us. We took advantage of that rare opportunity to get outside news from them. When talking with them, we came to know that during the campaign the Communists had kicked off against the bourgeoisie in the North after 1954, many people were robbed of possessions including money, land, houses... and forcibly sent to new economic zones such as this place. Most of them were Catholics from Thai Binh. We inquired about many aspects of their lives: the education of children, their religious practices etc... In response to questions on Catholicism, they said: "We don't have Mass here. We just say prayers. We baptize our own newborn babies. What we worry about most is how to find a Catholic for our children to marry."

For lack of a formal school, the villagers try to hire a number of tutors to teach their children how to read and write. As for living, from the beginning, they are free to clear as much land as possible to grow manioc, potato and corn. After five years, they have to pay tax on products. They work long hours for less. Their daily food is a mixture of corn, potato and (or) manioc. As rare food, rice is sold to them once in a while by the government. Sometimes, they go without rice for the entire six or seven months.

We felt free to talk with the villagers as long as the cadres spent their time flirting young girls. One day, an old man came. He was over 60, very thin but still healthy-looking, with sharp eyes. He looked around in the distance before approaching us and said: "We, the Northerners, have waited and waited, hoping to be liberated by you, the Southerners. And now, alas, we find you in this situation." He then turned away with downcast eyes. His statement came back to my mind again and again, piercing my heart. I felt sorry for the Northerners as well as for ourselves at the idea that we lost the war without even fighting, that we were defeated by the cunning, deceitful Communists and the maneuvering of international oligarchies.

The old man's remark is quite a blow to a number of politicians in the North as well as in the South who put their own interests above those of the country, thus causing sufferings to people and bringing the entire nation to disaster.

How important is the role of the country's leaders! They must be held responsible to our founding fathers and to the young generation of the country. May our country have patriotic leaders who are both talented and virtuous so that our people can enjoy a lasting peace and prosperity in the world's community.

Growing Green Vegetables
(at Camp Tran Phu)

The fever I just went through, definitely had a bad effect on my health. I was therefore assigned to growing green vegetables. The job was relatively mild, but it kept me busy all day. While working in the woods, although it was a very hard job, we had more time to relax and admire the beauties of nature. In the immensity of mountains and forests, we offered our praise to God, and glorified Him, the Creator of all things.

In order to grow vegetables, we needed to do various jobs: bedding, sowing, weeding and fertilizing... At harvest time, we felt the pleasure of having produced something to feed our friends. Some of us volunteered the humblest job for others. It was to make green fertilizer. Preparations were necessary. We went collecting yellow leaves and abandoned portions of vegetables. We also gathered small plants, weeds, cut them into small pieces and mixed them all in a big heap. We then covered the heap with mud, leaving some small openings for the air to circulate.

After about three months, the mixture would turn into good-quality fertilizer for vegetables. We then collected pig-waste, cow-manure and stored them at the corner of the garden for future use particularly for valuable kinds of vegetables such as *bách thảo*, turnips, onions, garlic...

The hardest part of the job was to carry buckets of putrid human waste and dumped the waste into a 2m wide and 1m deep hole full of water. The liquid must be stirred up thoroughly before fertilizing the way taught by Northern socialism.

One day, I was repeatedly scooping the dirty liquid to fill my buckets before carrying them to fertilize vegetables. At the sight of me in rubber sandals *(dép râu)*, a cadre shouted at me: "Mr. Que, why don't you take your sandals off and get down the hole and fill the entire bucket just one time instead of scooping up several times. It's much faster that way. You can never get the job done by doing the way you're doing. No wonder you lost the war and the South was slow to develop." After that, he kept standing there, staring at me, urging me to take off my sandals and wade, knee-deep into the dirty liquid. Although my body was smeared with human waste and the bad smelling became unbearable, I had to bend down to immerse the bucket in the dirty liquid. I tried my best to finish the job according to the way taught by Northern socialism. Actually, I did not care about anything. I worked away like a machine. I just wanted to get through with it unharmed as soon as possible. No wonder the North remains poor, I thought to myself, how can the country become strong and rich with this stupid kind of revolution. Back to camp, I had to crush fresh leaves in my hands to wash myself with, again and again, without ever getting rid of the bad smelling. It was quite an experience.

Ethics first, Literature second"
(at Camp Tran Phu)

Near the area where we grew vegetables, ran a rather large road leading to a school. The first time (and many times later) on the way to school, whenever boys and girls saw us, they shouted at us, trying to humiliate us and condemn us as traitors and lackeys of the American invaders. Some boys lay flat on belly, stretching out their arms toward us, pretending to shoot at us with an imaginary machine-gun while making continuous cracking sounds with their mouth. Others ripped their trousers open and urinated in our direction. The girls stood there, giggling with fun seemingly to approve of their ill-bred schoolmates. After that, boys and girls ran away, shouting and screaming aloud like crazy.

During the years of running schools in Saigon before 1975 (at least five schools, large and small), I did never witness such a show of bad behavior from the students. I really don't want to put everything in the same basket, but frankly speaking, the above-mentioned boys and girls did exhibit a scene of moral degeneration generated by the present implementation of an atheist revolution.

The more we moved to different camps in contact with cadres and their families, particularly when living with criminal prisoners, products of the regime, the more we worried about the future of the country.

During the time from 1954 in the North, and from 1975 in the South till now (1998), we distinctly felt obnoxious influences on every aspect, especially on culture and religion that had been brought upon our nation by an atheist revolution. In spite of separate efforts to improve the situation by individuals as well as by private organizations, good results have not been achieved yet as long as the atheist Communists are still in power.

Before becoming Communists, those people have been born Vietnamese, I believe, with Vietnamese blood in their veins. Therefore, we sincerely wish that every genuine Vietnamese should put the nation's interests above theirs and their party's. Together, we work to rebuild our country, to achieve the same goal: peace and prosperity for all people. That's the responsibility of every one of us.

My heart sinks whenever I think that those young people, still at the very early stage of life have been mentally poisoned by adults with ideas which foment hatred, rancor and generate a loose life. The young generation is the foundation of families and the future of the country. Therefore the motto "Ethics first, Literature second" must be a guiding light for them, at school, in family and society as well.

Mass celebrated in Privacy at the garden of White Radishes (at Camp Tran Phu)

Horticulture is indeed a back-breaking job, which requires a lot of manual work, but it is conducive to relaxation and peace of mind. Close to nature, we have the feeling we are collaborating with the Creator in growing vegetables and producing foods for our own living and others. We feel best at harvest-time when we get plenty of food for our friends and ourselves.

Early preparations were to be made for the next season even though the current season was not quite over yet. Therefore, we had to keep some reserves of vegetables for breeding purpose. During the year of growing green vegetables, at the request of cadres, we must put aside three beds of white radishes for breeding purpose. The breeder plants grew tall above head, thick with white blossoms, embalming the air with fragrance. The whole area came alive with flights of sparrows and insect-birds in search of food, with swarms of gorgeous butterflies and bees, busy sucking honey from flower to flower. The scene was so beautiful, just like in a picture.

One Sunday morning, I was given the job of watering vegetables. Happy with the assignment, I had the idea of celebrating Mass right in the garden. The job half-done, four catholic friends and I agreed to take a half-hour break for the Mass. We stole into the beds of radishes and started the Mass under the cover of white flowers. As man, king of the universe, the tile given by the Creator, I praised and glorified Him in such a beautiful way I have never had in my life. When the Mass was over, my friends left, leaving me alone in the garden. In silence, I prayed and experienced a wonderful time in the presence of God. Deep in meditation, I offered thanks to God. Anywhere, anytime during my priesthood, I am always protected in a special way by His providence. What He had said in the Bible, rang true to me: "Verily, I say into you. There is no man that had left house or parents, or brethren or wife or children, for the kingdom of God's sake, who shall not receive manifold more in this present time, and in the world to come, life ever lasting" (St. Luke, XVIII, 29-30)

Small wonder, Communist cadres often gave me ironical remarks, saying: "What a prisoner, called

'Father'!" Yes, I am a Father, called "prisoner". While they forbade me to be called "Father" and called me *"Thằng"* (appellation with no respect), my friends kept calling me "Dad". Father, Dad or *Thằng* or any derogative name is O.K. to me, as long as I do not lose my identity and they can never change my identity, I believe.

The Miracle of the Eucharist (at camp Hoang Lien Son 3)

Throughout the period of reeducation from South to North, most of my fellow priests and I, we were always protected, guided by God's love, and blessed with His permanent presence. I think the most special blessing we have received from God is that we have been able to celebrate the Holy Mass in privacy in camps. As a result, Catholic brothers had a chance to gain spiritual strength and devote themselves to the activities of the lay apostolate among fellow prisoners.

On Sundays, I usually celebrated Mass in privacy for my friends. In order to avoid the watchful eyes of informers, I must carefully change the site and Mass schedule, all the time.

One Sunday, after informing my friends of a new place and Mass schedule, I went to a brook to fix the broken handle of a spoon. At noon, it was getting hot. I sat by the cool stream, in the fresh air, busily tinkering with the broken spoon while by my side, some friends washed the laundry, happily crooning pre-war songs. Suddenly a Catholic friend rushed to me in panic. He said: "Don't you hear, Dad? The administration has called you several times through a loudspeaker. Hurry up! Go report or you will be in trouble." Indeed, I was too much pre-occupied with the repairs of the spoon near a noisy brook to hear the loudspeaker. I then hurried back to barrack put on a loose shirt *(áo bà ba)* and went to the administration office to report. The warden was standing in front of his office, waiting for me, with a black look on his face. As soon as he saw me, he said angrily: "You, Mr. Que, you are so insolent! I have called you several times and you don't show up." I answered: "Working by a noisy brook, I didn't hear, sir. I come here for report right away after being informed by a friend. Please, understand me."

He stressed each of his words: "Don't talk about understanding. You're a liar!"

"Sir, if you don't believe me, please ask the persons who are washing clothes by the brook."

After a moment of silence, he suddenly turned more furious. He pointed his fingers at me and shouted: "What do you have, pinned to your pocket like that? Show it to me!"

As if shocked by electricity, I automatically pressed the purse with my left hand and realized the Eucharist was still in my pocket. In a hurry for report, I had put on my shirt without taking the Eucharist off my pocket. In embarrassment, I reached out my right hand to unpin the purse containing the Eucharist and prayed in silence: "Oh Lord! Don't let them offend you. I cannot bear to see any sacrilege committed by them." I then unfastened my pocket, ready to show the container of the Eucharist to the warden, when for no reason, he surprisingly got dumbfounded with a waxen face. A long moment of silence passed before he could open his mouth and said with menace in his voice: "Next time, if you don't respond to my call, you shall be punished." He then turned me away.

Before leaving, I forgot to say "thanks" or "goodbye" to him. A number of friends came, asking me about my confrontation with the warden. I tried to calm them down and went back to bed in silence.

I was too happy for words. Since then, I have become deeply convinced of the actual presence of God in the Eucharist.

From my own experience, I often told my friends in the group of Eucharistic ministers to keep the Eucharist with care and reverence. Some of them were so fervent that they spent a whole hour during the night for the adoration of the Eucharist even after a day's hard work. I really admire their devotion. In return, God has blessed them with His abundant Grace and kept their families safe under His protection.

VI. PUBLIC SECURITY CAMP
PHONG QUANG, LAO CAI

One fine morning, we were ready for labor when the warden gave an order, saying: "Back to barracks to get packing, and line up in the front-yard!" The order caused quite a stir among us. I knew for sure we had to move and they were going to inspect our belongings again. I hurried to see some of Catholic friends I trusted, and told them to hide the Eucharist carefully while moving. As for me, I sought means to keep bread and altar wine in secret to take along.

It did not take me long to pack up as my life was kept simple with very few things: a knapsack, a bundle of bedspread and a blanket. When everybody had been in line, the head of the camp (with

147

the help of many additional cadres to speed up the inspection) said to us: "Today, you're gonna move to another camp. The revolution always tries to provide better and better conditions for your reeducation. The camp you're moving to is fully equipped with better houses and many amenities such as electricity, running water. Try your best to make more progress in reeducation, hopefully for an early return to your families." After that, he told the warden to divide us into groups for the inspection of individual belongings.

I learned from experience that we were robbed badly each time they searched through our possessions. They pretended to give us the feeling that they were helping us jettison extra load for a light voyage (sic!). We often saw them struggle for the stuffs we were not allowed to take along. They appeared very satisfied whenever they got something from us. But the more they satisfied their greed, the poorer of the poorest we became, alas!

The Communists always treated us in a "special" way, as we were priests. Therefore, on that day, one of the cadres inspected me very thoroughly. He told me to exhibit all my possessions in front of him and started to check them, one by one. I tried to keep calm, but deep inside, I worried about my vials of altar wine and prayed that they would not get caught. He took up every bottle of medicine and asked me to explain all the words printed in English or French on the labels. He paid special attention to a bottle of tonic. When he opened it up, and sniffed at it again and again, I took the chance to cleverly whisk my vials of wine into the pile of medicine, which had already been checked. I said to him: "In case you need this bottle of tonic,I can give it to you. Feel free to use it. It will do good to you and your family members." While he was still hesitating, I went ahead and dropped the bottle down the pile of my belongings already confiscated, intentionally for him to see, thinking it is worthwhile to lose a bottle of medicine and gain vials of wine in return.

As we were too crowded for a limited number of cadres, the inspection did not end till late in the afternoon. We were ordered to have dinner at once and get ready for the journey.

It was 5 p.m. when we started. The convoy of molotovas had lined the road, waiting for us. With packages, we climbed into molotovas, twenty persons per car. As usual, the same scene was repeated. We were hard-squeezed, closely covered and suffocated. As agreed, three of us (NVT, NDT, DNQ), we swore to always stick together. So we tried our best to get into the same car. Rev. N.V.T. looked very pitiful. As soon as in the vehicle, he felt dizzy and begin to throw up. I handed him a bottle of eucalyptus oil. The strong smell of oil blended with the offensive odor inside the car produced a third one (quid tertium) that was nauseating. Luckily, the convoy began to move. I composed myself and said some prayers, praying to God for a safe journey and for His protection against the unexpected happenings ahead. Since the day they took us to the North, we had to move continually from camp to camp. Wherever we went, we had to clear the woodland for growing potato, manioc, sometimes rice as the cadres usually said: "You have to build your own house and grow your own food." But as soon as we got the job done, we had to move to another camp, and again began to clear the land and grow the food, trying to practice what they had said: "You have to build your house and grow your food." Yes, it is our house and our food, but we are never able to use them. We came to know later that each time they exploited our labor to complete a camp, they sold it to the ministry of home affairs for the army-budget. How clever they are in realizing such a wicked scheme!

O Lord! Only you can save us from the miseries of a prison life. Have mercy on us!

In the camps at Hoang Lien Son (where inclement weather and unhealthy environment prevail), I had survived three accidents (as mentioned above) and witnessed the death of three friends. One of them was disemboweled by a fallen tree while at work. He was taken to the camp-infirmary to be roughly bandaged, but died from hemorrhage on the way to the Inter-camp.

Another one, in the same building with me, died from an unknown cause while sleeping during the night. He was found dead in the morning by a nearby friend when he woke up at the clang of the camp gong.

The third one died in a mysterious way. That evening when we were busy dividing our shares of rice, he told us to keep his portion for him and went back to barrack for the bowl he had forgotten to bring along. We waited and waited for his return. He still did not show up. After a long wait, we sent a friend to look for him only to find him lying dead on the ground in front of the barrack, with arms and legs, all curled up. At such a horrible scene, he screamed in panic, drawing a crowd to the scene. We then carried the body to the infirmary. After a day's hard work plus the sudden death of my friend, I could hardly swallow my dinner. I felt extremely sad. Back to barrack, before bedtime, I celebrated Mass with the attendance of two friends under the cover of a mosquito net. We offered thanks to God and prayed in particular for the friend who had just died.

Due to those sudden deaths, I often walked around barracks before going to bed to visit my friends and to make sure they were still alive. We merrily waved "good night" to one another. I also let my friends know that once in bed for about five minutes they would face towards my bed to pray and join me in celebrating Mass in secret, and to receive the Holy Communion by themselves right in their beds. We were thankful to be safe during the day, and prayed for a good sleep before a new day began, and for enough strength to walk the way of the Cross with Jesus to the end.

We did not reach the new camp until around midnight after many other vehicles had arrived before us. The camp-gate was well-lit with a sign which read "Camp Phong Quang". It was really a public security camp. Passing through the gate, we saw many rows of buildings surrounding a large campground. Everything seemed very much in order. High walls topped with barbed wires for prevention of escape enclosed the camp all around. Here and there watchtowers loomed high with strong searching lights sweeping the night-sky back and forth. Armed guards were in a state of watchful readiness. In comparison with other camps, this one was quite a difference. In camps managed by the Army deep in the woods, we felt better with more breathing space, in spite of hard labor. Here, in a public security camp, our living conditions were better while living in buildings, enjoying electricity; however, we felt limited and restricted in every way, and especially insecure among public security agents who always kept watchful eyes on us.

The warden escorted forty of us to a room in the left wing of a building. Both sides in the room were lined with bunk beds, leaving a passage in between. In spite of limited space, the room must accommodate forty people, anyway. I chose to sleep on "the upper level." Dinner rations were distributed to us. The food was salted tofu. The first dinner was not bad, giving us the feeling of being welcome. Actually, the food standard the camp authorities were trying to achieve, could not satisfy our permanent hunger. We heard that camp Phong Quang was rather well organized. Officer Qui, the camp-head, was a benevolent person. He took good care of us.

That night, I slept rather well in a warm room. Before going to bed, I did not forget to celebrate Mass in privacy to offer thanks to God for a safe journey after an exhausting day of travelling. There must be more difficulties for us to face in a public security camp like this one. May the Lord give us enough wisdom to cope with new circumstances and new people. We must be on guard all the time, as public security agents were said to be nasty and wicked persons.

At around noontime of the following day, all of us must gather in the meeting hall. Major Qui, head of the camp, well-dressed in public security uniform studded with all kinds of medals and military decorations gave us a friendly talk: "You have been officially put under the management of the public security service. Here, you must keep the rules and regulations of the camp and make great efforts to study. As a representative of the party and the Government, I'll do my best to nurture an environment favorable to your reeducation, so that you will become good citizens and return home to be useful to society. If any of you have difficulties to face and urgent needs to fill, feel free to let the management know. Your problems will be resolved at once. We will see to it that you will go to work in a few days. Meanwhile, the wardens will guide you for the settlement of a new life and for a general clean-up in and around the camp. You hear me?"

"Yes, we do." We usually answered that way just for form's sake.

When the meeting adjourned, we all went back to our rooms.

In connection with a number of friends, we came to know more about camp Phong Quang.

The camp was very large with three divisions: A, B, C. Division A where we were living, was the main camp. Camp B and C were reserved to detain political prisoners of the South. We did not know how many of our friends had been there, but we did know that former police officers and intelligence agents had been in camp C long before us. Later, whenever we had the opportunity, we tried to contact them for more information.

After more than a week in camp Phong Quang, our group started the first day working outside the camp. We were divided in different groups for different jobs: construction, making brick and tile, weaving, growing sugar-canes, producing molasses, transportation, growing green vegetables... Many groups (including mine) were assigned to clear the land for growing manioc, corn, potato, even sowing rice-seeds.

**Wearing near-sighted glasses
is a sign of disrespect.**

Whenever going out for labor, we had to walk in two straight lines, well-dressed with camp-distributed uniforms, a pair of sandals with front and back fasteners to hold feet tight, with *nón-cối* over head and tools in hand. When we passed through the gate, the group leader shouted out for us to take hats off and reported to the guards, the group number, the number of persons present and the number of persons absent (due to illness). One of the cadres on duty wrote down all the information on a list before letting us go. We started walking when a cadre shouted, pointing to a person wearing glasses. "Stop! Who are you? Why don't you take off your glasses in front of us. You show no respect for the cadres." (They thought glasses might be equipped with hidden radar or radio to send out and receive secret messages.) All of us were very surprised at what he had said. Our friend answered: "I'm near-sighted, sir. I need glasses to see." We did not know if the cadre really understood what "near-sighted" meant. He then softened his voice saying: "Next time, remember to take off your glasses. Now the group can go." We did not want to get into trouble, so I (like those who wore glasses in my group) readily took glasses off whenever passing by a cadre. What had happened, turned out to be a laughable topic of the day during our conversation in the labor field. We felt sorry for him and his ignorance.

Deadly Manioc

Arriving at the labor field, our group began to climb up the surrounding hills for the clearing of land. Each of us was assigned to a lot about 10m long and 3m wide. Some had to work harder than others, depending on the number of trees and bushes in their lots. No matter what, each person must finish clearing a lot in one day. The norm was becoming more difficult for us to meet as in the public security camp, we had to stop working at noon and walked in line back to camp for lunch. We did not return to work till 2 o'clock in the afternoon. That way, we had more time to rest, but must work shorter hours for a time-consuming job.

One of the hills got bare in three weeks. The time came to cultivate the soil for planting manioc. While digging, hoeing, weeding and breaking land into beds, we discovered bulbs of manioc left behind under the soil. We hurried to report that lucky event to the warden, and with his permission, brought a large quantity back to camp. We then boiled the bulbs of manioc to eat as a kind of nutritious food for health improvement. The warden had carefully told us to soak the bulbs in the water for a long time before boiling them and to let them cool down before eating. We did as advised and everybody in our group was safe.

Two days later, after dinner when everybody had been back to buildings in silence, ready to sleep, we heard a sudden cry for help from a nearby building.

It was about 10:00 p.m. After a moment, cadres arrived. We saw bright lights all around and heard shrieking sounds of opening locks but did not understand what had been happening.

The next morning when we started for labor, we noticed the absence of people in the nearby building where the accident had occurred.

A few days passed before we came to know the whole story: people in that group also found left-behind bulbs of manioc. They happily brought them home, boiled them and ate them at once without a chance of being cautioned like us. The quantity of manioc was large enough for each person to have a share up to one kilogram or more. Some ate a whole portion at one time. If unable to eat it all, they were happy to share with others. After meal, everybody got more or less intoxicated. They felt dizzy, nauseated, some to the point of vomiting and having diarrhea. One of them was a big guy. Due to excessive hunger, he ate so much, much more than his share that he collapsed to death beyond any measure of rescue. The whole group had been food-poisoned, indeed. At the news, the camp chief hastened to have molasses brought to them, saving the remaining lives in time. The sweet stuff had a detoxifying effect on the poisoning manioc. How simple the treatment! The big guy however was not lucky enough to be treated that way, alas!

Thanks to the experience, the entire camp was cautioned to be very careful when eating the manioc left behind for a long time. As for me, to be entirely safe, I did not touch that kind of manioc any more. Hearing of the bad news, fellow priests and I concelebrated a Requiem Mass in secret for the dead man.

Improved Cars

While detained in camps run by the army, we had heard a lot about "improved cars." In the North, those who could afford such a car, numbered among the rich. In my imagination, an improved car must be a scientific invention of high technology, which aroused curiosity.

One day, people in construction group were pulling across the camp ground a cart with some wooden boxes in it when a friend in my room cried out: "There comes an improved car! Who wants to see it, hurry up!" At the call, I rushed to the window to see what the car looked like. Oh my God! Is that an improved car, I asked myself? It was quite like an ox-drawn cart except for a smaller size with an iron-frame, two round shafts also made of iron, and two bicycle-like wheels with solid rubber tires. It appeared heavy and hard to move due to lack of ball bearing in the center of the wheels. As galvanized to the trunk, the shafts could break easily, and technically speaking, were inferior to those of an ox-driven cart. It could however carry heavier loads thanks to a pair of shafts running the whole length of its trunk. I woke up from the illusion that socialism had attained a high level of technical science. How gullible we were! We had been misled so far by Communist cadres when they boasted of the Communist world. According to them, Russia, East Europe and China are all super and well-developed countries. How clever they are in deceiving others.

Superior Fuel

As a priest, I need this kind of fuel badly for daily Mass to glorify God and bring His grace down on earth. Since the day I was secretly provided with a bottle of altar wine for the first time by a brave Catholic cadre living a strong faith, I shared this kind of fuel with my fellow priests and told them to use it sparingly. As for me, I only used a drop of it for each Mass. In the long run, however, the entire content was drained off, drop by drop. In the embarrassment of how to get some more wine, I happened to meet a catholic friend in a building near the meeting hall. During our conversation, I came to know in that building there was a priest named Hien, a member of the Congregation of the Mother coredemptrix (CMC) who often celebrated Mass in secret. I told my friend to find out if Father Hien was able to give me some supply of this superior fuel. My friend promised to help. A few days later, during the camp assembly in the hall, my friend came and secretly handed me a phial of wine, saying: "This is Father Hien's gift with best wishes." I happily concealed the phial under my shirt. The assembly was about the news of the expansion of Chinese troops. I did not care to hear them. My mind was haunted by the new gift. I became more convinced of the Divine Providence. God is indeed a merciful father who always takes good care of his children, particularly those like us suffering a miserable life. He managed to provide me with a phial of wine through Rev. Hien.

Back to my building, the first thing I did was to convey father Hien's regards to my colleagues and to share with them some altar wine I had just got to make sure every of our groups could regularly benefit from the Holy Mass.

From then on, Divine Providence was more than just what I believed. It became my intimate, living experience of what God had done to me during the 13-year period in Communist prisons.

O Lord! I'm grateful to you for a boundless love you have reserved for me.

November 17, 1997

VII. CAMP BA SAO, HA NAM NINH
OR CAMP CHINE, DAM DUN (HNN)
OR CAMP NAM HA (HNN)

Division B

We had heard about the expansion of Chinese troops for several months. We did not even know for sure that they were friends or foes. There must be something unusual, we thought to ourselves. Each time cadres talked about China, their faces turned red with anger. Here at Camp Phong Quang, thanks to the prestige of Major Qui, the camp-head, the atmosphere was somewhat relaxing, although we were restricted in many ways. Life became a little bit easy with regular work schedule and some facilities. In addition, there were not so many difficulties for us to conquer as in army-run camps. But wherever we were, we were treated as prisoners, anyway. We readily accepted our fate hopefully to be set free soon.

As they claimed the right to put us in prison, so we had the same right to get out of it. My friends had one time discussed that matter with me, asking for my opinion. China is only 12km away. The terrain around Phong Quang appears favorable with less rugged mountains and more accessible forests. There is also a bridge crossing a river along the border. Furthermore, with the help of a friend named N.A.P, a native of Nung tribe in the North, who seemed to know the terrain rather well, we could make it to China easily. Once there, we were certainly safe, as China was then being in conflict with Vietnam. Some decided to go ahead with their plan, in spite of my disagreement. I only prayed that they would succeed as planned. "Man proposes but God disposes." Their dream of escaping could not materialize because we were ordered to move again.

While in the camps run by the Army, we had moved several times with no problem at all. Under the management of the public security service, however, each time moving, we were required to be handcuffed as dictated by law. After all packages had been brought up to molotovas, the cadres ordered us to get in two lines. They then used a 8-shaped handcuff to tie the right hand of one to the left hand of another. I shared a cuff with Rev. P.Q.T. As a result, wherever we went (even to the restroom...), we had to go together. That was the first time I was handcuffed since the day I reported for reeducation. At first I felt a little bit unusual, but the feeling later

162

became something cumbersome and deeply humiliating. In a closely-covered molotova, Rev. P.Q.T.
and I said the Rosary together, praying to Jesus for
a safe journey and for a new strength to carry His
cross. (We heard cadres telling to one another that
a car accident had happened along the way.) It was
almost dark when we reached camp Nam Ha, division B in August, 1978. It was a small camp nestled
at the limestone mountain slope in the city of Ninh
Binh. The camp was rather dirty, sloppy and loosely
organized. There was a well in the middle of the
camp-grounds for washing. At the destination, we
were happy to meet one another, forgetting all the
miseries during the last 24 hours of travelling. After
dinner, we went to bed early. I celebrated Mass in
secret at once, with the participation of former major Dich, an elder brother of a Redemptorist living
in France. We thanked God for a safe travelling,
and for a happy reunion with many friends considered killed during the last battle in 1975. We also
prayed for enough patience and endurance to cope
with all the difficulties ahead. Feeling heavy in the
head, I took a pill of quinacrine for prevention of
malaria fever. I usually did so whenever moving to a
new camp, and it proved to be very effective.

The way in which a gift is given, is worth more that the gift itself

On the feast of Assumption, when I went with
others to take food for lunch, I heard a call. I turned

back and saw Rev. Hien, the one who had supplied me with altar wine at Camp Phong Quang, Lao Cay. We waved to each other happily. He said to me: "After receiving your lunch, remember to come back. I have something for you." I nodded without even knowing what "something" was.

On the way back, I stopped by father Hien's room. He was curled up in a hammock due to limited space in the room. Seeing me, he reached into his inner pocket and took out a tube. He opened it up and said: "On the occasion of the Assumption, I give you some sweetener crystals. It's good to mix them with salt in a cup of water to eat with." I reached out for them with a short "thank you" and left. Back to my room, I did as told. The mixture was indeed very tasty. I crossed myself and began to eat my lunch. Lunch meal that day turned out to be a banquet to me in honor of the Virgin Mary. Father Hien and I, we sympathized with each other easily through priesthood. That was the first time in life I knew the taste of sweetener; thank God, thank mother Mary and thank you, father Hien for your gift.

I am told that after being released, Father, your health is deteriorating. I'm writing these few lines in your remembrance. May God and Mary accept your self-sacrifice and bestow upon you many blessings. When you return to your Heavenly Father, don't forget to tell Him about the wine and sweetener you have given me.

I lost 32 kgs.

At army-run camps, they worked us very hard, continually without a day of rest, even when we were ill. They sought every possible way they could imagine to exploit us physically. During the three years we had worked like crazy, to exhaustion I might say, just for a certificate of merit as worthless as a mere piece of waste paper. "After a period of good reeducation, you will be released." That was their promise. But we just could not understand what a good reeducation should be. How clever the Communists are in playing tricks on us! Their skill of deceiving people is beyond compare.

We had been in Division B, camp Nam Ha for more than two weeks, but no labor-date was mentioned. Idle time was boring. But to me, to do nothing at that time became a privilege, because I felt my health noticeably declining. In army-run camps, we had toiled and moiled more for less food under unfavorable weather conditions. After many days of fever, and without enough food, my health was really going to the dogs.

Upon arrival at camp Phong Quang, we got a general medical checkup at a hospital in the city of Lao Cay. Every one of us was startled by the bad results. As a strong man, I used to work tirelessly all day long. At the time when I reported for reeducation, I weighed 75 kg. But then, my weight was only 43. I lost 32kg in a few months. Health condition of some was even worse than mine. We felt almost permanently dizzy due to hypotension. With graying hair, and a stooping figure, we aged beyond recognition.

The central ground of camp B was not very large. We went there everyday to talk to one another or just to walk around. Present at that time was a person who used to work with me at the special military zone of the capital. Yet, he was unable to recognize me, although he knew that I was there. Thanks to a friend's help, we finally met. We were moved to tears at the pitiful sight of so much physical change in each other. We agreed to meet again the following Sunday for a longer talk.

Camp A

Until then, we understood the reason why we did not have to work while at camp B. It was because they planned to keep us in Camp A, not Camp B. At about noontime that day, we were ordered to move to camp A, around 1 km away. The journey was relatively easy. We weaved our way between mountains and saw Dam Dun nestle among beautiful boulders in the distance. After a while, one of us looked forward, saying: "It must be camp A over there." Built on the limestone mountain's slope, the camp looked quite colossal with barbed-wire-topped high walls all around, and with watchtowers standing firm at four corners. The more we approached the camp, the more uncertain we felt about what was going to happen in the future. Our fate resembled that of a mouse caught in the claws of a cat. They could do us whatever they preferred. I quietly said

166

the "Our Father", "Hail Mary" and "Glory be to the Father", praying for sufficient wisdom to cope with new difficulties in a new circumstance.

Camp Nam Ha with a big gate, high walls and a very large yard looked so peaceful amidst romantic natural surroundings. It was ironic that it turned out to be a prison. That was one of the camps run by public security service notorious for severity. Of three divisions A, B and C totaling 15,000 political prisoners of the South, division A was the largest with the presence of virtually all the representatives of the entire former government of the South, I might say, Prime Ministers, Congressmen, City-Mayors, District-Chiefs, religious leaders, members of political parties, high-ranking officers of the army, military police, security and intelligence agents, not to mention Fulro members and fighters for the recovery of national independence who came late...

At the camp gate, we had to get in line and exhibit our possessions for them to check before being allowed to enter the camp. I was lucky to have a cadre who checks my belongings just for form's sake. Without asking me anything, he just swept his hands over various articles carelessly, telling jokes sometimes for sympathy, and finally said: O.K. I politely thanked him before going. To my observation, he might be a Southerner who had regrouped in the North, a member of the Liberation Front. As you know, after the South was liberated, the Front fell into disgrace. Was it because of being disillusioned that he sympathized with us? I offered thanks

167

to God for that easy-going cadre and for the safety of my wine and bread. What God's providence had permitted to happen to me and to other Catholics in camp, was very meaningful. There was reportedly a priest who had been here before us, but had been transferred somewhere else due to a mishap during Christmas season. And now we had a total of six priests, instead. With such a great number of priests in camp, God must have the intention to do something special to us. I will report to you, my readers, on major events in the following pages, so that, together we can praise His love for us.

The First Sunday Mass in Secret in the Campground of Nam Ha

7,800 was the number of political prisoners at Camp A, Name Ha. It was indeed the largest of all. The sense of togetherness seemed to be a great joy for us. The problem however was sometimes not as simple as it appeared to be. The reason is that as a former chaplain chief of the special military zone of the capital, I used to have a lot of connections. During the first week, I tried hard to find out about the general situation in the camp, particularly about the spirit of catholic friends. The first person I met was colonel Truong Dinh Lieu, a former associate of mine. We were so happy to meet again. He told me his wife was dead. Thanks to the information gathered from many, the first sad thing I knew, was that there were informers who served as "antenna" for

Communist cadres, who often played prisoners against each other, thus causing division and mutual suspicion among us. Secondly, selfishness prevailed among prisoners for lack of mutual help. The rich bribed cadres to win some favors, whereas the poor lived a lonesome life.

Thirdly, there were no religious activities among Buddhists, Cao Daiists, Hoa Hao followers, even Protestants to support their followers' spirit. All these made me sad.I have to do something, I thought, to help them, especially my catholic brothers.

I went from building to building, trying to contact catholic friends. With the cooperation of those serving as liaisons, I planned to celebrate the first Sunday Mass right on the campground for as many Catholics as possible.

That Sunday, after dinner when everybody spilled onto the campground for conversation before bedtime, as planned, standing in front of the meeting hall between two friends who acted as guards watching around for any mishap that might arise, I took off my hat as a sign of performing the sacrament of reconciliation for everybody. I then put the hat on to start the Mass. Here and there, catholic people turned toward me in secret participation. I took off my hat again as a sign of consecration, and then put the hat on, telling them to receive the Communion (with bread ready in their hands). I prayed in silence, and lifted up my hat to bless all the participants. The Mass ended.

In spite of the crowd and the presence of armed security guards, the Mass liturgy had been going unnoticed.

That first Mass was quite an encouragement for Catholic friends. They began to feel more secure spiritually in the midst of their religious leaders. Since the day I succeeded in organizing the celebration of the first Sunday Mass, I came to know that other priests also had their own groups. They all, however agreed with me when I suggested that each priest should take care of a building he selected to avoid possible conflict. As for me, I chose the farthest building near the main gate.

We did our best for good results. Each group was in charge of a favorite subject: Bible study, adult religious education, lay aspostolate training, liturgy etc... Each of us primarily focused on the catechetical instruction for the catechumens, getting them ready for baptism. As a result, we met people who wanted to be baptized anywhere we went in the camp. Glory be to God!

The spirit of great unity

While caring for the Catholics, I did not forget those of other religions. Before 1975, I used to work with Buddhist and Protestant chaplains. Therefore many of my friends were Buddhists and Protestants.

Present in Camp Nam Ha were 10 former Buddhist chaplains and 5 Protestant chaplains. They had been here long before me. But their spiritual influence was not very strong. People were low-spirited, depressed and selfish. They just lived for themselves, without caring to think of others. As spiritual leaders, I thought together we can make the difference, if we try to be more active.

One day, after work, as usual I took a bath before going to the food distribution center for my rice-portion. On the way, I happened to meet a Buddhist monk I knew. When I posed the problem for him, he answered: "Let me contact my colleagues first." I tried to encourage him: "We used to care about our brothers before, you know. Now, in this difficult situation, we have to do something for them, hopefully to lift up their spirit." Not all of ten monks readily accepted my suggestion. Two or three younger ones, however, were full of enthusiasm. My Buddhist friends began to think of observing death anniversaries, and holding secret worship service according to Buddhist rituals.

I thought they should have a high spirit and a strong belief first. Once equipped with those spiritual tools, they would be able to cope with the trials of life.

Minister Dieu Huynh

After the Buddhists, I came to my Protestant brothers. I met Minister Dieu Huynh one evening when we went to take our food share. He was still very young, about 30, with a good tan and a small frame, yet gentle and joyful. When I shared with him my ideas, he responded with reservation: "How can I do now, Father. I don't know anybody here." I answered him: "I have quite a few Protestant friends. If you agree, I can introduce them to you." He nodded in agreement. After leaving, we made an appointment to meet again, the following day. I kept the appointment and brought to Minister Huynh Dieu a Protestant. They shook hands with each other and both seemed very happy.

Since then, Rev. Huynh Dieu began a really active life for the propagation of faith and succeeded in baptizing many people. According to Protestant ritual, baptism is performed by immersion. Therefore, I sometimes saw Rev. Huynh Dieu take people down the swimming pool in the camp, or down a river, a brook on the way to labor field for baptism. He steadily maintained his zeal ever since. In 1982, we left camp Nam Ha for camp Phu Ly, and then Thanh Cam. By the end of 1987, when I returned to Camp Nam Ha, Catholic friends introduced to me many neophytes. Rev. Dieu Huynh also came to me, gratefully informing that he was still as enthusiastic as ever in spreading faith among his friends.

I can never forget those heroes of faith in my life. Glory be to God!

Feeding Visits

Back to Nam Ha, we were able to gather a lot of information. We came to know the reason why we had to leave Army-run camps for camp Phong Quang under the management of the public security, and then from Phong Quang to Nam Ha.

According to 1979 news reports, Vietnam invaded Cambodia in a scheme to topple Polpot government in order to form the Indo-Chinese Confederation (of Vietnam, Laos and Cambodia). The audacious invasion plan of Communist Vietnam did much harm to the international relation. It particularly offended China that was then sponsoring Kmer Rouge forces. China wanted to teach Vietnam a lesson by threatening to occupy six cities along the border. For fear of being invaded,Vietnam troops were sent partly to Cambodia for additional help, partly to the Northern border in an apparent attempt to stop the advance of Chinese troops into the six Northernmost cities of Vietnam where most political prisoners of the South were being held. To avoid being kept hostage, all prisoners must be transferred in a hurry to camps located in the Red River delta area under the management of the Public Security service.

After a few days in Camp Nam Ha, our group was doing the cleanup around the cadres' residence when we heard a cadre cursing in a loud voice in front of his friend: "Damn it! Chinese guys acted damn fast! They broke into our camp as early as 4 in the morning, shooting wildly, leaving us no time to get prepared. Suddenly awakened in awe, I ran for life, only in shorts. The camp was disastrously destroyed. Even electric posts were torn down. Damn it! I was almost killed. It was so... so scaring! Besides injuries, we suffered some casualties. Luckily, nobody was kept hostage."

The news of China's expansion was true. Chinese troops withdrew right after the destruction was completed. They did not bother to stay. They just wanted to teach Vietnam a lesson. A few days later, the camp head had all of us rallied around him and proudly boasted of "our victory over China," saying: "After defeating three capitalist leaders of America, France and Japan, our invincible troops have once more succeeded in chasing the Chinese expansion troops out of our country." We just sat in silence, winking at each other in irony. If only the cadre of camp Phong Quang I just mentioned, had been present, he would have told the real situation for everybody to know. The more I reflect on that event, the more convinced I become of Divine Providence. Otherwise, we would have died gradually in the jungle. Luckily, we were not forgotten by the world. Under the international pressure, the Communists were forced to release political prisoners. In addition, they felt the need of our families' cooperation to feed us. Eventually, the policy of "feeding visit" was born.

One day, we were playing chess in our building when two lieutenant colonels from the ministry of the Interior came to visit us. They inquired after our health and then discussed about the living conditions in the camp. One of them said:

"As you all know, our country has just been liberated entirely. There remain, however, quite a few thorny problems for the revolutionary government to solve. Our nation is still poor. More food is to be produced to meet the needs. Thanks to the benevolence and leniency of the government and people, you are granted the privilege of reeducation. The problem is too big for the government to solve unless your families cooperate in feeding you. So, your family members will be allowed to bring some food along whenever they come here to visit you. Such a policy will foster a good re-education. As a result, you will be able to go home soon to help the government build a strong socialist Vietnam."

We were happy to hear the news. However, I thought, it is only a policy of "passing the buck." Our families will become poorer because of us, whereas the Communists credit themselves with being humane. Since then, camp authorities allowed us to write to families for a feeding visit.

I was not recognized by my brother

The first time my family visited me was the Labor Day of 1979. The road to the reception center was very hilly. I had to stop three times for rest before reaching the destination, only some hundred meters away. After reporting to a cadre, I stood waiting for my family members to appear. After a long wait, my younger brother reported to the cadre, asking: "I need help, sir! Why has my brother Que not come yet?" The cadre answered: "Don't you

175

see? Your brother is there." My brother then rushed to me. We embraced each other with tearful eyes before the bewildered youngest child of my brother. "O God! You have changed so much in just a few years. I can't recognize you." He said, "My son and I saw you coming but we did not think it was you." I kissed my nephew, and together we went into a designated room for a talk. In a low voice, my brother continued: "My son and I arrived here yesterday afternoon. I have already bribed the cadre with enough gifts. He seems very nice to us." I felt free to talk continually with my brother for thirty minutes as allowed by law. I was informed of the general situation of my family. My parents were in good health, but they missed me day and night. I extended my best wishes to everyone in the family. I only requested some necessities for a prison life, especially what I really needed for my health. The food my brother brought that first time was only 5 kg. He handed the gift to me, saying: "Our primary goal this first time, daddy said, is to get to know what you really need, so that family can feed you more adequately in the future. We always keep you in our prayers."

The time ran out. I said good bye to my brother Ngo Van Tri and nephew Tuan before going back to camp with a load of 5 kg of food. On the way back, I found it easier to go downhill, though.

When checking my gift at the gate, the cadre said to me in a threatening voice: "I know you're the one who often loiters around buildings to talk with your friends. If you are caught violating the rule one more time, feeding visit shall be cut off."

To jump out of the frying pan into the fire

Nam Ha was labeled an international camp. Near Hanoi, the camp had a better opportunity to welcome the visitation of many international delegations. Each time visitors came, only a limited number of prisoners was chosen to appear for show while the rest were whisked away to a hiding place, for fear that unwanted realities would be exposed to guests by the secret revelation of reactionary elements. I was always chosen for hiding. In 1981, the camp was honored with the visitation of a delegation of the Amnesty International. We were told that Premier Pham Van Dong had allowed the delegation to see whoever it wanted to. Delegation members were three celebrities: a doctor, a high-ranking officer and a priest.

The priest was a redemptorist named Gerard Gagnon. The Vietnamese called him Father Nhan. He was well-known for lecturing in Vietnamese and well-versed in the stories of Kieu, Chinh Phu Ngam and Cung Oan. He was also my former teacher of philosophy. As a member of the delegation, he chose to speak only English or French, with the help of an interpreter. Father Nhân understood everything spoken in Vietnamese, even a soft whisper uttered by cadres. Upon entering the meeting hall, the delegation was greeted by a music band. The Communists wanted to prove that they still cared for culture and arts even in prison.

A song just ended when Father Nhan recognized an acquaintance. He burst out in Vietnamese: *"Anh Tín, anh có nhận ra tôi không?"* (Do you recognize me, Mr. Tín?) While in embarrassment, colonel Tín (a former military band conductor) did not know what to do because the camp regulation strictly forbade him to speak with anybody in the delegation, father Nhân added in Vietnamese: *"Tôi là Gagnon đây! Sao anh quên tôi nhanh thế?"* (I'm Gagnon. Why do you forget me so fast?)

Mr. Tín answered briefly: "I do remember you.", stealthily looking around for fear of being heard by the cadres. Everybody, including the cadres was puzzled at a Caucasian's fluency in Vietnamese. Since then, Father Nhan began to talk in Vietnamese with prisoners as well as with the Communist cadres. When visiting the infirmary, the delegation went from bed to bed, inquiring after each patient's health. That day, the infirmary was kept clean, well organized and fully equipped just for show. A can of Longevity milk was on each bed, seemingly ready for the patients to use. During his observation tour, Father Nhan inadvertently said: "to jump out of the frying pan into the fire." By that, he meant: "Stop that kind of deceitful show, please! We know it all!"

It was certainly true. After the delegation left, they had all those cans of milk collected and taken away. They just wanted to torture us by whetting our appetite without caring to satisfy it. The same show was repeated when the delegation arrived at the kitchen and saw two dangling killed pigs, which gave the impression that those pieces of meat were for prisoners. In reality, they were health-improving portions reserved for the cadres, as the pigs disappeared right after the delegation's departure.

We did not have lunch until after three o'clock that afternoon. We were taken in hiding to Camp B. Back to my building, when hearing my friends' report, I regretted not being able to meet my former teacher Nhân. He showed a special affection for Vietnam. His main purpose when accompanying the delegation to Vietnam was to help release political prisoners.

In 1993, when settled in the U.S. I intended to go to Canada to see him, but my plan could not materialize because his Heavenly Father had called him home.

May he pray for Vietnam, a nation he had served in love for virtually all his life.

Colonel Ho Tieu

As priests, we served everybody without distinction. We were ready to help anybody who came for advice, for sharing their feelings about a letter just received from family, for medicine, for whatever they needed. To us, love comes first. It is through love that our relationship becomes smooth and easy. In the camp circulated a book of New Testament published by the Catholic Chaplain Directorate. For fear of being confiscated, the book was separated in chapters for easy circulation among Catholics and non-Catholics as well. Whenever I saw someone read the New Testament, I encouraged him: "This is a source of strength, a guiding light in dark times of tribulation."

Of non-Catholics interested in reading the Bible, two captivated my attention most: Mr. Thieu, the youngest colonel of the Army of the Republic of Vietnam and colonel Ho Tieu, former commander of the Special Forces. Both of them later wanted to be converted to Catholicism. Colonel Nguyen The Trinh was in charge of religious instruction. As for me, whenever available, I could do some more help. Preparations for baptism required a whole year due to very few occasions for us to meet in camp. Furthermore, it was an important matter in life, I would like to give them more time before they were able to decide. When the time was ripe, I would see them one by one. Colonel Thieu said to me: "Father, after studying Catholicism, I love it and very much want to become a Catholic. But I don't think I'm ready for it, as long as I still nurture in my heart a deep rancor for the Communists, which is against God's teachings. Therefore, give me some more time. When I am released, my family members and I will be ready." I shook hands with him in admiration for his conscientiousness.

Mr. Thieu and I were released together in 1988. But I have never had a chance to meet him again, even though we both are in the U.S. now.

Now back to Colonel Ho Tieu. He was so happy when I told him to get ready for baptism. The long-waited day was about to come. He continually urged Colonel Trinh to get him to be baptized as soon as possible. Whenever we talked about religion, I saw the reflection of a strong faith and the fire of love for God in his eyes. Colonel Trinh would be his Godfather who was going to choose a patron saint for him. But he wanted to be put under the patronage of Saint Michael, known to him as an Archangel when he was commander of the Division of paratroopers at Ngo Dinh Diem time. So, I chose to baptize him on the feast of Archangel Michael (Sept., 1981)

That day, we did not have to go out for hard labor, thanks to the sudden visitation of a delegation. Mr. Trinh, some others and I, together, we went into the cultural house to baptize Mr. Tieu. We were sitting around a table, apparently reading something when I started to perform the sacrament of baptism on him. To close the ceremony, we said in a soft voice the "Our Father", "Hail Mary" and "Glory be to the Father", thanking God for having admitted Mr. Tieu to His Church. We also asked Mother Mary to protect him, and Archangel Michael, his patron saint, to travel with him always during this journey on earth.

After that, we said: "Congratulations!" and shook hands with him. Suddenly, I burst out: "If only we could have a day off and raw meat to celebrate this happy event with Mr. Tieu!" I did not have to wait long, because right after that, a cadre came, announcing: "Today, you don't have to work and you will have meat to eat, too." Everybody applauded at the news and shouted with joy in celebration for Mr. Tieu. A miracle just happened before our eyes, I might say. We had lunch together, that day, happy to see our dream come true.

Since the day Mr. Tieu was baptized, we noticed a big change in him: more amiable, more helpful, especially more eager to encourage people around him to read the Bible as a source of joy and consolation.

In 1982, all the priests were taken to camp Me, and then to camp Thanh Cam, Thanh Hoa for solitary confinement. Since then, I did not meet Mr. Tieu for years. By the end of 1987, when I returned to camp Nam Ha, looking for him, my friends reported: "Last year, he became so seriously ill that the revolutionary Government sent him home. And we have no news of him ever since." Not being able to find him, I felt rather sad, but strongly believed that as a man of faith, he was always loyal to God in any circumstance. I then said a special Mass in privacy for him.

I was set free in early 1988. I spent a month in the North, visiting my native village and places where childhood memories were still dear to me before returning to Saigon. The first thing in my mind was to look for Mr. Tieu's whereabouts. Through contacts with colonel Trinh, his Godfather and Rev. Le Trung Nghia, a redemptorist, I came to know he was living in Go Vap district.

I made a trip to Go Vap and stopped at a beautiful villa. The main building was occupied by the Communists and they just allowed him and his family to stay in a shabby shed and a car garage at the backyard. At his sight, I took a sidewalk right into the yard where he was lying in a hammock. He was about to get up, but I stopped him, telling him to remain lying in place. He told me everything since the day he came home. Beside his poor health, religion had become a big family problem for him. His wife and children continually attacked him, forcing him to give up God and return to Buddha. But he decided to cling to his new faith at any cost. As a last resort, his family invited a Buddhist monk trying to win him back to Buddhism, but in vain. He had met God and had seen His light. He could not step back. Everyday, he went to a nearby church for Mass and talked confidentially with the pastor about his difficult situation for support and consolation. The pastor promised to pray for him.

One day, as if braced with the Holy Spirit, he said to his wife: "Dear, have all the children come here. I need to talk with everybody in the family, now."

Are these the last words of a person who feels the end of his life is drawing near due to a terminal disease, she thought to herself? Thinking so, she readily complied with his request. That evening, with everyone in the family around him, he said: "Since the day back home from prison, I have been feeling very happy when living with you. Thank you all, my dear ones! You have taken good care of me. So far, I have done nothing harmful to you and family except the problem of religion. As you know, personally I respect freedom of religion very much. I always let you go to pagoda, to participate in Buddhist charitable organizations and keep relation with monks and nuns. Once again, I thank you for your continued support and prayers, especially for feeding visits during my miserable days in prison. You don't have the right, however to deprive me of religion freedom. During thirteen years in prison, I had the opportunity to live with people of different religions and study the Bible. After long days of reflection, prayer and deliberation, I have come to the decision of following Jesus Christ. He is really the light, the purpose of my life. I need your understanding, please!" After a short pause, he turned to his wife and continued with more determination: "Excuse me, my dear,I can leave you. But I can never leave my God."

Since that day, nobody dared to bring up the matter of religion again. Life in family ran smooth as if nothing had happened. I am thankful to God and mother Mary for having a friend of strong faith like that. He really deserves to be called a child of our martyred forefathers.

After I had met Mr. Tieu, Rev. Nghia and Mr. Trinh went to see another friend, leaving me alone with him, and promised to return to pick me up. The following day, I went early to see Mr. Tieu again, with some books for him to read. "Whenever you need me, just give me a call," I said.

Released in 1988, I chose to stay in the North for the celebration of the Lunar New Year with family. I did not return to the South until the beginning of 1989 to celebrate my first Tet festival in Saigon. On the first day of the New Year, a great number of relatives and friends came to greet me, wishing me a happy New Year. In the afternoon, when I was receiving guests, a person hurried to me, his face pale from fear, saying: "Father, Mr. Tieu is dying in Nguyen Van Hoc hospital, Gia Dinh. He wants to see you." Shocked by the news, I left everybody to look for Rev. Nghia and Mr. Trinh. We went to the hospital at once and found him in a state of coma. His wife was weeping at the corner of the room. When I put my hand on his head, miraculously he opened his eyes, looking at me as if he were waiting for me. I bent down over him and whispered to his ears: "Are you ready?" He gave me a wink as a sign of readiness. I then anointed him and blessed him for plenary indulgence. After that, he became unconscious again. I said a few words of consolation to his wife and left.

The next day, I went to the hospital early in the morning to see him. He had been transferred to a nearby room. He seemed better than the day before and was aware of my arrival. I asked him: "Can you receive the Holy Communion?" He nodded in agreement. When I gave him the Eucharist, his face brightened with happiness. He held my hand tight, repeating words of thanks. I said to him: "I might come back tomorrow for you to receive the Communion again." He did not show any sign of response. I blessed him, said goodbye to his wife and left.

On the third day of the New Year, so many well-wishers came to me that I had to rearrange my schedule in order to be able to see Mr. Tieu in the afternoon. But I did not have the chance to see him any more, because at around 3 p.m. one of his family members let me know that he had died. The news left me speechless for a while. I then asked my guests to excuse me and went looking for Rev. Nghia and Mr. Trinh. We arrived at the hospital in no time, and found out that Mr. Tieu had died at noontime. His body had been taken to the mortuary and Mrs. Tieu had also left. She seemingly could not afford to bring him home. Understanding her difficult situation, I rented a taxi, and with the permission of the hospital, brought his body home. I performed the body-blessing rituals right at the mortuary where his body was still lying on a camp bed. The funeral service according to Catholic ceremony would take place later at a Church. As his family members and the majority of relatives and friends were Buddhists, Mrs. Tieu wanted her husband's official funeral service to be held according to the Buddhist tradition. At the time Mr. Tieu's body reached home, a number of monks in saffron yellow robe had been present. I said to Mrs. Tieu: "I have brought his body home for you. It's up to you now to do whatever you see fit for him. As for Catholic ceremony, I am in charge. You don't have to worry. My sincere condolences to you and your family. If you need something, please feel free to let me know."

On the way back home, Rev. Nghia, Mr. Trinh and I felt very happy, believing Ho Tieu's soul had been saved.

When blessing Mr. Tieu's body, I opened his eyes for examination and saw his face radiant with joy and peacefulness. He must have met his Father in heaven.

At the news of Colonel Ho Tieu's death, people from neighboring parishes including priests and sisters came to visit his body and pray for him. The dean priest in the area of Go Vap also came to share the grief of the bereaved family. He even offered to celebrate a Requiem Mass right at Mr. Tieu's home, if possible.

As Buddhists, Mrs Ho Tieu and family members did not know how to respond to such a kind offer.

They came to me for advice. After talking with Rev. Nghia and Mr. Trinh, I decided to concelebrate Mass with the dean priest as celebrant. I let Mrs. Tieu know my decision, and with her, set a date for the Mass.

The Mass for the soul of Michael with the concelebration of 5 priests took place at Mr. Tieu's home with unexpected solemnity. My eulogy in which I praised him as a living testimony of faith, brought many to tears. Among a large attendance were congressmen, generals, high-ranking officers, paratroopers, members of Special Forces, various organizations and many others. The main house, even the front yard and backyard were crowded with people. His casket was kept in the house for four days. During that time, Catholics and Buddhists took turns to come and pray for him. He was buried right at the backyard. On the funeral day, I was intentionally absent for fear that my presence as a priest, might cause some inconvenience to Buddhist monks. The next day, I went to visit his tomb. It was well-designed by Mrs. Tieu, herself.

I always keep Mr. Ho Tieu in my prayers. While preaching, I often mentioned his name, considering him as a wonderful example of Catholic faith. May God have mercy on him and bestow many of His blessings on Mr. Tieu's family.

Mrs. Tieu has been reunited with her children in the United States. They are now living together in the city of Cerritos, California.

Celebrating the Silver Anniversary
of Ordination to the Priesthood in Prison
(Sept. 8, 1956 – 1981)

Before 1975, I used to attend many priests' anniversaries of ordination: Silver Anniversaries, Gold anniversaries and Diamond Anniversaries. Their solemn celebrations sometimes lasted for tree consecutive days with the participation of many people including the nobility, high-ranking officials in the Government, army officers etc... This is a blessing from God to be thankful for, I thought.

If the event of April 30, 1975 had not happened, I could have celebrated my silver anniversary of ordination to the priesthood the same way. (The council of Bishops was about to appoint me general director of chaplains replacing Rev. Cao Duc Thuan when his term was over. The news came from Bishop Le Van An, in charge of all the chaplains in Vietnam. His purpose when breaking the news was for me to get prepared.) At that time, I had connections with over ten thousand parishioners in the area, not to mention 40 executive committees in various Army units under the direct control of the Special Military Zone of the Capital.

Learning from experience, I realize that God never lets me enjoy the fruits of my work. I readily accept it because I think it is better to work now while I am still young for the future generation to enjoy. That point of view of mine was realized when I left Vung Tau for Saigon. While reorganizing the new place in

Saigon, I was suddenly appointed director of chaplains. I joyfully left everything behind for the new position. I thought I could go anywhere God wanted me to go. As a priest, I was called to serve. My life was on the high rise when the event of April 30, 1975 happened. I decided not to go abroad, but to stay with my brothers and sisters. Now, kept in prison, I accepted to suffer, even to die with my friends. Therefore, when my silver anniversary of ordination to the priesthood came, I just got my soul ready in silent celebration according to God's will..

To Build dam Nam Ha, Ba sao

The camp-authorities took advantage of the great number of political prisoners to build a dam (as big as the Red River dam) leading from Ba Sao to Nam Ha. The dam could run several kilometers. What a clever idea!

We broke into groups for the job. As intellectuals, we used our mind to organize and work in an effective way, with some digging, others scooping the mud, while the rest standing in line carrying the muddy land piece by piece. It was really a back breaking and dirty job especially during the rainy season in Winter. Months and months of working hard without getting much done proved that the project was unrealistic. We often comforted one another jokingly: "Try to get the job done in order to be released." By that, we implied we can only finish it in hundreds of years, until the time when our bones turn into ashes and our tombs are nowhere to be found. Indeed, the project was finally left unfinished.

Men to replace buffaloes to till the fields

Another special job for the prisoners to do in Camp Nam Ha was to cultivate the soil for rice planting. No matter how hard it rained and how cold it was, we had to wade into the mud to cut wild plants and weeds for room to grow rice. Oh my God! There were so many blood sucking leeches that we bled everyday. We often joked among ourselves: "This is exactly a blood-debt for us to pay." After the clearing came the plowing. Everyone of us thought that in the North, under socialism, there must be many buffaloes, oxen or at least tractors for farming. In reality, there were only two buffaloes in the camp. As a result, we, mostly congressmen, generals, colonels must assume the job of buffaloes. One person held the plowing machine while two others in front of him, bent down striving hard to pull on a stretch of rope with one end fastened to the machine and the other one running across their breasts. It was a really pitiful sight to look at! After the plowing, the harrowing must be done the same way. Never in my life had I felt so humiliated. In the name of reeducation, we were treated no better than animals in a society known to the Communists as well-developed with high technology.

During harvest time, we experienced a sense of

relief and joy at the idea that so much of our hard labor had borne fruit. The ripe ears of rice reminded us of the farmers' labor. We then understood the deep meaning of a popular saying: "Oh Heaven! Let it rain upon us! For water to drink, for fields to plow, for bowls to be filled with rice, and for straw to cook our food." Our farmers always turn up their faces to Heaven as a sign of thankfulness.

According to what camp authorities had said, rice we produced was intended to augment our food ration. But the truth was we permanently ran short of rice and we had to eat potato and sorghum, instead. Without feeding visits from our families, many of us including me must have died long time ago.

I considered my current labor as a way to prepare for the celebration of my silver anniversary of ordination to the priesthood.

During a quiet moment of prayer, I said to God: "To celebrate my anniversary, I offer you, O Lord, what I have, particularly my present sufferings. I owe you a lot, O Lord! Being ordained to the priesthood, I started spreading the good news for a few years. After that, I was appointed teacher in the Juvenat of the Congregation of the Redemptorists at Vung Tau. In 1965, I served as a chaplain for Vung Tau area. After a short training period (1969 – 1970) in the United States, I returned home to serve at the Special Military Zone of the Capital. And now, I am kept captive in a Communist prison with my friends. Thy will be done, O Lord! Looking back at my 25 years of serving as a priest, I realize a continued supportive love you have had for me during the ups and downs of my life. As a human being, I have strengths and weaknesses. In either case, you always stand by me. Whatever happens to me, is according to your will, I believe. O Lord! I don't want to be on my own. I pledge to put myself under your control, so that you can act within me. All the good work I have done is yours, not mine. Mine are only defects and blunders.

How can I thank you enough on this special day of my anniversary. With Saint Mary's advocacy I would like to sing "Magnificat" in praise of you. I sincerely pray for my parents, relatives and friends, for the great family of the Redemptorists, for my benefactors and all the persons I have served and will serve. I ask you to give them abundant reward in return for what they have done to me. Please, help me faithfully fulfill my pastoral duties in your name.

I also pray for my present situation. Please make me a proof of your love among my friends. And if you will, I can die in prison as an ultimate sacrifice to you for your glory, in retribution of my sins, for my beloved country, even for my pitiful Communist friends."

I continued to harbor those thankful feelings in my heart until the day of my silver anniversary of ordination to the priesthood: Sept 8, 1981, also the birthday of Saint Mary. In the beginning, nobody knew my anniversary except my fellow priests and two others: former colonel Truong Dinh Lieu and Colonel Nguyen The Trinh. But after a day of hard Labor, representatives from most buildings unexpectedly came to greet me. I had nothing to treat them. I only shook hands with them in appreciation and asked for their prayers. That evening, my fellow priests shared dinner with me at Rev. Tran Van Thong's place for the celebration of my anniversary. The affection they showed me was not only a proof of our solidarity but also a good example for our neighbors. After meal, Rev. Trung (also a Redemptorist, my one-time classmate, but ordained 2 years after me) came to my room, and together we celebrated a Thanksgiving Mass. I could never forget that evening when the celebration was very simple, but it bore the deepest meaning of love God has for us through the Holy Mass anywhere, anytime forever and ever. Thank you, Lord, for having chosen me, your humble creature as an intermediary between you and humanity to say: "Do this in memory of me", to declare your glory and bring your grace down on earth.

While I was in bed, a friend suddenly appeared, asking me: "Father, why so many people from other buildings came to greet you, today?" You have something special, haven't you? Touched by his sympathy, I frankly answered: "Today is my Silver Anniversary of ordination to the priesthood." He shared his feeling with sincerity, saying: "You should not keep it secret. Your joy is also ours." He shook hands with me before leaving. After a few minutes, he came back with a significant number of friends to greet me. Luckily, I still had a box of Chinese tea and a pack of cigarettes. We drank tea and smoked while talking confidentially till very late before going to bed.

Later on, it came to my knowledge that many other priests also reached their 25th anniversary of ordination, but to them, it was only an occasion of quiet remembrance, not a celebration as solemn as mine. I further realized a special love God had reserved for me. O Lord, I would like to lift up my cup of thankfulness to you for your abundant love.

Food from Love

"Noblesse oblige" (Nobility obliges.) Fed by their families, many of prisoners became rich, so to speak. They often rallied for parties. They sometimes talked about politics, too. I was invited to some of those parties. Later, realizing that they had gone beyond limit, I avoided them. To tell the truth, I felt very disappointed at the idea that all those precious foods, resulting from the daily savings coupled with so much sacrifice and hard work of their loved ones, were being wasted in a foolish way. Some of them even traded food for cash to gamble. Such bad manners could not be tolerated. To my knowledge, a great number of suffering wives were behind their imprisoned husbands and children. Their job went double.

At home, they toiled and moiled day and night for enough food to feed their young children and babies, and also their husbands in distant Communist reeducation camps. A girl just married some months before the fall of Saigon, was soon separated from her husband detained in a reeducation camp in the far North. Alone at home with no job, she was forced to live with a married Communist cadre for money to buy food for both herself and her husband in prison. As I knew, the husband was not prodigal. He did not know anything except to admire his faithful wife's love and care. The heart-breaking story came to be known only after he and I were released, of course. It was, alas, too late to do anything about it.

It was such a tragedy, but many of those "so-called" rich, remained insensitive to others' misfortunes. As for us, from poor families, we only received gifts once a year, and later, once every two or three years. Satisfied with the scarcity of gifts, we still considered ourselves fortunate enough. Without monthly feeding gifts, many of poor friends had to use whatever others gave them. Such a pitiful sight made us think of lonesome people such as those who used to live in sister-run orphanages. On special days like Tet Festival, Christmas, Easter, All Saints' feast, feast of the Vietnamese Martyrs, patron saints of soldiers... we sometimes organized meals for them. We formed an organizing committee to make necessary preparations. Everybody readily participated in the cooking. Members of the committee pooled their own foods, with the contributions from many others at my request. Many times, we could not eat it all and there were some left-overs to go, too. Everybody enjoyed the food without reservation because they all knew the food was coming from our love.

How wonderful the gift of sharing!

Waves of Feeding Visits

At the beginning, feeding visits were few and sporadic. Family members went not just with gifts, but particularly to explore the real situation first, so that they could tailor the feeding pattern to the needs of their loved ones. Later on, visits took place more and more often, with loads after loads of food supplies. The quantity of goods was so great that the camp must use trucks instead of ox-carts for transportation.

According to Communist propaganda, the South of Vietnam had been impoverished by merciless American exploiters. Therefore, the Northerners had to snap a grain of rice in half for the starving Southerners. And then, after the invasion of Cambodia and Laos, they again repeated the same way of saying: a grain of rice must be snapped in three for both Laos and Cambodia. But the truth was absolutely contrary to what they had said. After Vietnam was reunited, communications became easy with all parts of Vietnam, which gave the Northerners a chance to see with their own eyes and found out that the Southerners were much more civilized and wealthier than they are. "How do you think about the South?" I asked some cadres and particularly a security officer who just came back from Saigon. He spoke his mind, saying to me: "The South is really wealthy and beautiful." I posed one more question: "How do you compare Saigon with Moscow?" He answered: "Saigon is definitely better than Moscow in Russia" and then added: "Especially the girls, they are so lovely, courteous, their voice so mellifluous!" That officer was still single, of course, and had been to Russia and East Europe before.

After April 30th, the entire regime of the South was subjected to the system of reeducation, and the Southerners began to bear the brunt of financial difficulties. They wanted to get out of the country by any means, even by risking their own lives. Luckily for those whose relatives made it to foreign countries. At the news of feeding visits allowed by the Communist government, people living abroad began to send home gifts and money to help their loved ones financially and also to support those detained in reeducation camps. Since then, gift sending and receiving services were booming both abroad and at home. In 1988, when released back to Saigon, I could not believe my eyes when I saw towering piles of gifts from abroad at Tan Son Nhut airport. Those gifts had saved hundreds of thousands of people from starvation while indirectly pumping up the economy of Communist Vietnam.

A two-apartment storehouse was getting filled with gifts once a month not only for Camp A, but also for camp B and C, and for camp Me, Phu Ly as well. The store-keeper, a female cadre, was promoted to an even higher position in spite of the fact that she had shamelessly stolen what she was supposed to keep (I will come back with her story, later.)

The Communist scheme of feeding visits won them credit for being humane, but at the same time became their own petard they would be hoisted with. The wealth of the South was beyond their imagination, and the mutual love and affection among Southern family members exceeded their expectation. The Communists were further surprised at the fact that feeding visits continued to happen waves after waves as long as reeducation camps still existed. In reality, the Southerners did not need a half or one third of a grain of rice from the North as the Communists had said. The great quantity of gifts began to puzzle Communist cadres from camp-heads to armed guards, whetting their appetite for material things and raising in their minds many unanswered questions about the Party and the government. They certainly did not want to stay poor. But how to get a better life, they thought, if not by stealing or forcing those good things out of prisoners. As a result, cadres were more satisfied while prisoners could breathe again. That was the current situation at Camp Nam Ha.

The main target of the Party and the Communist

regime was to liberate the South and turn it into a socialist country, but the result went to the contrary. Most cadres sent to the South had become corrupted and turned capitalist or at least preferred capitalism to socialism.

It was a life-time experience since 1975 for every patriot (Communist or not) to learn from and to think about in order to avoid disaster for the country.

A Champion for Running Around

Since the movement of feeding visits started, the situation in camp Nam Ha changed for the better. While we were fed by our loved ones, we in turn, fed the cadres in one way or another, thus winning some of their sympathy and respect. In that new atmosphere, I often stole into nearby buildings to visit others, sharing gifts and clothes with them, or providing medicine for the sick, even celebrating Mass in secret or giving religious instruction to those who wanted to convert to Catholicism. After a hard work's day, I usually took a bath, got dressed and disappeared in no time. I had a trustworthy friend who took care of my rice-portion. Whenever I came back at night, my dinner had been ready on the bed. Therefore, I could venture out almost every evening. If someone wanted to find me, they'd better go to hidden corners in the buildings, in the kitchen, to isolated bushes or to places conducive to confidential talk or religious instruction especially on Sundays and Holidays.

One Sunday, I went to a building near the main gate to celebrate Mass in privacy for former colonels. On the way back, when I just stepped out of the building, I was caught red-handed by Mr. Luc, a cadre on duty. At my sight, he shouted: "Stop, Mr. Que! What are you doing here?" Even though I did not want to tell him everything, I had to stop and answered him: "I come here to visit my sick friends, sir." He directed his wrath at me, saying: "You are a champion for running around. You have connection with everybody. You shall be disciplined for having broken camp's regulations." Misfortune never comes alone. When he saw the gospel I had borrowed from a friend for the Mass still being held in my hand, he asked in a loud voice: "What kind of book you have there? Let me have a look!" Though in panic, I could do nothing but hand the sacred book to him. Reading the large print on the cover he recognized the book, which made him angrier. He shouted again: "No wonder, you go to propagate faith. Now go to my office and wait until I am back. I've got to talk with you." I restlessly waited in his office, knowing for sure that something serious was bound to happen. Discipline was unavoidable. My friend's book could be confiscated.I made up my mind however, not to say anything about the secret celebration of Mass. I prayed particularly to the Holy Spirit for enough strength to face at least 15 days of discipline. I had waited only 15 minutes before Mr. Luc came back. As soon as he arrived, he shouted angrily: "You, a champion for running around. If you're running around, I'm gonna discipline you and see if you can kick off that bad habit of yours. Go back to your room for a report of review in which you must clearly state the purpose of your trip to the former colonels' building and the reason why you keep the book. It must be confiscated now." I pleaded in vain with him to have the book back. He stressed his voice: "You, a champion for running around! I'm gonna teach you a lesson."

Back to the building, I finished the report in 20 minutes, admitting my guilt, and cleverly implying that I wanted to have the book back, without however mentioning the purpose of my trip to the colonels. When I submitted my report, cadre Luc received it without saying a word.

I went back to my room, thinking that discipline could not be avoided. I made necessary preparations for that day to come, thinking to myself: It's good to have the experience of being disciplined at least one time for God's sake. I asked my friend to excuse me for the lost book, and promised to buy him another one. Those who knew my problem came to console me and pray for me. Days and days passed without me being called to discipline, which surprised me. I had to wait a long while before daring to venture out to visit the former colonels again and celebrate Mass for them.

At Camp A, we had to change rooms every six or seven months. The warden must be replaced at the same time. Before going, Mr. Luc told the warden who was going to replace him: "Pay a special attention to Mr. Que. He is a champion for running around." Hearing that, I could not help laughing. But deep inside, I prayed that I was able to always practice what that surname meant for me to do for the benefit of my friends' souls.

Back to Camp Nam Ha late in 1987, I had the opportunity to meet Mr. Luc again. He had been married. That time, he showed me more sympathy and respect, calling me "*Cụ*" (appellation given only to a respectable senior), would you please give me this one, give me that one..." I was pleased to give him whatever I had, as much as I could, not because he called me "*Cụ*", but rather, because I was sensitive to his needs and the poor living conditions of his family. Actually, there were quite a few cadres who knew how to behave; and in return we tried to treat them accordingly. As was the case with a female cadre whose husband got killed in Cambodia, leaving her behind, with babies to feed. But his meager pension was unable to sustain her and her babies. Considering her pitiful situation, fellow priests and I, we pooled our savings to help her buy a bicycle as a means of living. That's the reason why each time we move to another camp, we often notice eyes wet with tears among the cadres. To us, love is what matters. Therefore we try to share with them our love, as of Catholic people, especially love coming from God.

Who have more influence?

Living in a community of prisoners, we slept together, ate together, worked together. But whatever we do, wherever we are, we—as priests—have no right to lose our identity. Priesthood is for ever (Sacerdos in eternum.)

In a camp, the more the merrier; Prison-life, however, became more complicated because of the crowd. Profanities for example were what we had to hear almost everyday. Psychologically speaking, profanity is good in the sense it helps many vent their pent-up emotions, thus releasing tension. The presence of a priest, however, might help reduce the number of foul-mouthed people.

One evening, after Mass and the Rosary, when I went visiting a friend at a far corner of the room, a number of people rallied, telling dirty jokes, at times bursting in laughter. At my arrival, one of them thrust his elbow at his friend's side as a warning signal, saying: "Hey! Watch your mouth! Father Que is coming!" Everyone in the group stopped talking. Still, I heard a voice saying: "Father... so what? I don't care!" However, when I got onto my friend's bed, I heard no more obscene words.

One day, at break time, camp authorities came to visit us right in the labor field. Coming to my group, they seemed very nice and smiled easily. I took that opportunity to voice my concern: "Gentlemen, to my knowledge, a number of cases are being considered, and some of detainees have been released. As for us, the priests, nobody cares to study our cases. A person seemingly oldest in the staff answered: "As you know, the revolutionary government is very lenient. We can release Prime Ministers, generals, anybody who makes progress in reeducation. Back home, ministers have no government and generals have no troops. As for you, the priests, we have to be very careful when thinking of releasing you, because back home, you still have too many children (meaning parishioners). This requires more, much more time for reeducation." After they left, I kept thinking how much is "more" or "much more." What do they mean by that? The Communist policy is to destroy religion, especially Catholicism. It is therefore not easy for them to release hundreds of priests and other religious leaders.

My case is really a miracle. They wanted us (priests) to live in exile in the far North, in camp Cao Bang, Quyet Tien (Camp Heaven Gate) until we die. God has saved us, I believe. "Man proposes but God disposes." The Communists want to kill us, but they can not go against the will of God.

O Lord! You are to be praised and glorified for ever and ever.

This is the wedding ring for you to keep, my dear!

Imprisonment is suffering in itself, let alone deportation far from home. During the first few years, as planned by the Communists, we were isolated in the jungle, completely cut off from families, relatives and friends. Such a solitary, lonesome life led to complete despair easily, causing some to seek escape by any means, even by vandalism and by stealing guns to fire at cadres. Since the day the revolutionary army invaded Cambodia, and Chinese expansion troops taught Vietnam a lesson, in prison we hungered for news. Waves after waves of news made us really confused.Therefore, we started the movement of secret letter-writing. We sometimes bribed cadres to be able to send a letter home for outside world information or to stay with our family member longer than permitted, sometimes as long as 24 or 48 hrs during feeding visits. We went even further by buying a used radio from a cadre. The radio had only one channel. Still, we could hear news from VOA and BBC. We had to take turns to listen to the radio and spread news to others. The radio must move from building to building to avoid being discovered by informers. The radio broadcasts helped us keep abreast of the most recent information about Vietnam and the world, every night. Now, we were "full" of news, not as "hungry" as before. Everything went relatively smooth for about a year until the day all the priests had to move to camp Me, Phu Ly.

The staff and wardens knew by hearsay that a secret radio was circulating in the camp. They tried to search for it, but in vain. The informers were so active that the news of a secret radio reached the

Ministry of the Interior. Not trusting the camp-authorities any longer, they suddenly sent a group of inspectors to the camp very early in the morning. The inspectors rushed into our room. After ordering everybody to vacate, they called us back to the room, one by one to check our belongings. All of us were scared to death, for we just listened to the radio that night. I knew for sure that it was still in the room. In case the radio was discovered, we would be in big trouble. We prayed under our breath so that we would be out of danger. They carefully checked the belongings of each individual, one after the other. When finished with the inspection, a person could go back in line in the yard for another's turn. Every one of us knew that the only way to escape was how to hide the radio in a pile of items already checked. Luckily, one of our friends had succeeded in doing exactly so.

Not being able to find the secret radio, the officials of the Ministry of the interior left, very angry. We were safe, finally. What a relief! The recent event however, still made us tremble with fear. Thank God for having saved us. We decided to destroy the radio, anyway, leaving no evidence at all. It was so dangerous to play with fire.

After the officials' failure to find the radio, camp-authorities seemed happy as they proved to the Ministry of the Interior that they had fulfilled their duties in keeping law and order in the camp. To be honest, we as prisoners had defeated all three of them: The Ministry of the Interior, the camp-staff and some unknown wicked informer. A few days later, the staff sent for a number of suspects for investigation. Some of them must be transferred to another camp. A former police major named Han caught their special attention. He had an intuition that something must be happening to him. So, before leaving, he went over to a neighboring building to see a close friend of his, saying: "If I die, keep this wedding ring for my wife, and tell her that I say "farewell" to her.

That night, he followed a cadre to camp B where he was tortured to death. The next morning, it was rumored that Mr. Han had hanged himself in the discipline room. We really did not know if it was true or not. But we did know for sure from experience that such kind of rumor was heard again and again each time a prisoner happened to die in the camp.

Like everybody in the camp, my heart broke at the news of Mr. Han's sudden death. All of us missed him very much. That very day, I celebrated Mass in privacy for him. I always remember him and his wedding ring. It was so beautiful a marriage-love.

November 24, 1997

VIII. CAMP ME, PHU LY

The peaceful atmosphere at Camp Nam Ha was conducive to religious and social activities. I worked with so much zeal for the propagation of faith that I forgot I was a prisoner. Is it true that after the event of the secret radio and Mr. Han's death, and that since the day Communist Vietnam invaded Cambodia, many international delegations came visiting concentration camps where human rights were explicitly violated, and forced Vietnam to solve part of the problem concerning political prisoners? It was rumored that camp Nam Ha would be put in the hands of local authorities. If that's so, some political prisoners would be released while others would be brought back to the South, in camp Ham Tan and that all the Catholic chaplains would be concentrated in camp Nghe Tinh and Thanh Cam. Actually, the Communists kept a close watch on only Catholic chaplains. Protestant and Buddhist chaplains were allowed to mix with laymen.

All the above-mentioned rumors became a reality. All of us, Catholic priests, were ordered to move to camp Me, Phu Ly where we were kept in solitary confinement, in other words, we were not allowed to get in touch with anybody including cadres, except wardens. They did not want anybody to be influenced by us. It was however a blessing for us as we had a long-sought opportunity to live together.

At the news of moving, I hastened to see my friends, encouraging them to maintain a spirit of mutual help, to keep spreading faith, and to get involved in social activities. Before leaving, I shared with them some of my consecrated bread.

A non-Catholic colonel came to say good bye. He held my hand tight, likely to weep and said: "Do you really go, father, leaving us alone?" I tried to calm him down, saying: "My fellow priests and I, we are here no more; but our heart and mind are always with you all. We always remember you in our prayers.

After he left, I returned to my room and got packing at once

A Lady from Hanoi

At about 3:00 p.m., six of us were transported to Camp Me. All of us seemed reluctant to leave camp Nam Ha, not because of its relatively relaxing atmosphere, but because we had no more chance to serve deported political prisoners during the most miserable time of their lives.

Arriving at a river, we had to wait for a ferryboat while cadres took a breather in nearby houses. We stood along the riverside, thoughtfully watching around in silence. When a ferry from the other side of the river arrived, we saw a luxury car with five well-dressed passengers in it: four gentlemen and one lady. They must be influential people in the government, I thought. After they had set foot on land and were waiting for their driver, the lady approached us and asked: "Are you political prisoners from the South?" We answered with a nod: "Yes, we are." She then added: "Honestly, I feel so sorry for you. What a shame! We have got peace; and our country has been unified. Yet, they still maintain this kind of policy. Why don't they release you, so that you can contribute more effectively to the development of our country?" We said, "Thank you" in appreciation of her sympathy. At someone's call, she waved good bye to us before getting into her car for Hanoi

It was our turn to embark. During the voyage, I kept thinking of the lady's words of sympathy. Right! if the policy of reeducation had been terminated soon, if the Communist government had carried out the true meaning of reconciliation, our country would have not been in such a bad shape. Everyone hoped that after national re-unification and recovery of peace, the whole nation would enjoy happiness and victory. Alas! The truth was totally different, the entire country was doomed to interminable deterioration and destruction.

We reached camp Me at around 4:30. The camp was located by a large river. It was shadowed by leafy trees and bamboo hedges. The area reserved for solitary confinement, was surrounded with high walls capped with barbed wires, secured by two watch-towers. The camp-head, a major, greeted us right at the gate. He was a lanky man, somewhat advanced in age, known by hearsay to be the kindest of all in inter-camp Nam Ha. He was appointed to this position apparently for semi-retirement.

We were then taken to a secluded area. A room deemed to be large enough for six people. This was a seclusion camp. As the name implies, it was cut off from the surroundings, far away from everybody. We started a new life. At night fall, I celebrated the first Mass in the camp with the concelebration of other priests. With many concelebrants, I had the feeling we glorified God better, and the Mass brought more Divine grace to those who were turning to us from other camps.

Huong Tich Apricot Wine
Kept in solitary confinement in Phu Ly, I had a good opportunity to live together with other fellow priests. But we just sat around, doing nothing. Since idleness engenders boredom, we asked the warden

to give us some work to do.

A few days later, we got an order to grow green vegetables in the yard of the discipline hall behind the secluded area. We planted all kinds of vegetables according to seasons. They praised us for maintaining the garden well, which yielded good quality produce.

Like in Camp A, cadres understood and treated us rather well. We helped them a lot, and in return, they also helped us get the necessities of life.

We had been working on green vegetables for several months when one day the camp-head visited us and let us know that he would need help in making Huong Tich apricot wine. In order to do the job, we had to go to the cadres' residential area, but we were not allowed to talk with them except when the need required. Actually, our only job was to clean and rinse out the bottles. They trusted us because they knew we were conscientious workers who not only did the cleaning well and fast, but also did it with great care. We tried not to break the bottles as other criminal prisoners often did, thus saving a lot of damage for the camp. We were sometimes assigned to cork up the bottles and stick labels on them. We were praised for everything we did. While bottling wine, we were allowed apparently for reward, to drink as much as we preferred, provided we did not get drunk. We also tasted some, but nobody liked it. Later on, whenever we had a chance, we bought apricot honey and mixed it with rice-liquor as an invigorating drink for future use.

The method of making Huong Tich apricot wine required a lot of effort as it was made by hand. The wine, shipped from Da Nang was up to 80° strong. After being mixed and diluted into apricot wine, its intensity was down to 15°. Frankly speaking, if you knew how the wine had been made, you would not bring yourself to buy it for use. The wine was intended to sell to the Northerners. It could not, therefore compete with any kind of wine made in the South.

Group 20

This group was characterized by its young members. They were partly Southern politicians, partly fighters for the recovery of the nation captured after the South had been liberated. Full of enthusiasm, they got involved in all kinds of activities, especially in eradicating injustices which often happened in the camp. Informers were their primary targets. They could not condone the behavior of someone known for sure as an informer. One day at camp A, a former colonel was assaulted on the way to the kitchen during the night. They rallied around him, threw a blanket over him and hit him almost to death because they knew he was an informer. Luckily, an armed guard who happened to pass by saved him. Sometimes, I had to interfere. I advised those young men not to go too far. Such a heavy-handed treatment of informers might result in death, which would threaten their own lives, and consequently turn them victims of their zeal. Everybody knew that the Communists often played one prisoner off against the other. The enthusiasm of those young people in-group 20 had actually done much harm to them. The most tragic result was that the entire group was sent to camp Me for disciplinary measures. We did not know how to help them, because when we arrived at Camp Me, all of them had been put in discipline rooms.

One day, a criminal prisoner in charge of carrying rice to discipline rooms for those young men, handed me a piece of paper saying that they were suffering from serious dysentery, in need of medical care. I planned with my fellow priests and threw packets of antibiotic to them through a hole in the toilet room while working in the garden right behind the discipline house.

On Sundays and Holidays, I often went to the garden, apparently to look for worms, but actually to whistle holy songs, encouraging those prisoners to share the spirit of the Holidays or to follow the Mass ceremony.

After having been in camp Me for more than a month, we heard that former lieutenant Hong died of dysentery in the discipline house for lack of medicine. When I saw his body being carried across our area, I raised my hand to bless him and went back into my room to hide my emotion. The Mass I celebrated that day was specifically for him. That young officer had won my heart since the day we were together in camp A. As a young Catholic officer, he was admired by many for his character and talent, which guaranteed him a bright future. He was particularly good at performing music arts. He had composed a song entitled "Back to Saigon", reflecting a deep love he had for mother Vietnam. I really admired that young man. May he soon enjoy Heaven's delights in the Holy presence of God. Dear Hong, I miss you.

A Beautiful Woman from Saigon

I had a special affection for the members of group 20. While in camp, they often came to me for advice, or just for a visit. Even now, back to normal life, some of them in the United States still maintain a good relationship with me. How can we forget one another after years and years of sharing moments of joys and sorrows in prison, and helping one another to survive in difficult times.

The leader of Group 20 was Mr. Luong Viet Cuong. He was a former teacher of mathematics at a Redemptorist school, on Ky Dong street. He was captured in Saigon as a fighter for the restoration of the country, and after a while, taken to the North to be detained in a discipline room at camp Me. He got married and had the first daughter not long before being arrested. Being left alone at home with her baby, his wife got the idea of doing business for living. She waited for the baby to grow old enough for grandma's care, and then traveled back and forth across the country as a migrant vendor, selling goods to customers from South to North. She took advantage of her business trips to visit her imprisoned husband. Thanks to her success in business, she was able to visit her husband every month, with tons of gifts, thus enabling him to breathe more easily even under severe disciplinary measures. As a young, gracious and beautiful woman, she easily won the affection of cadres of all ranks, male and female as well.

Before going to camp to visit her husband, she usually made up her face carefully and dressed up after the latest Saigon fashion, thus causing the Communist cadres to stop working in order to treat their eyes for a while. They wondered how such a beautiful woman could take pains to go a long way from South to North just to visit her husband. They must certainly admit that the South was rich, and at the same time marveled at the Southerners' beautiful marriage life.

In the United States, I have had a chance to visit Mr. Cuong and his wife at their home in San Jose, California. We were very happy to meet again. The meeting further consolidated the friendship that had existed between us since the day we were in prison.

A Catholic Captain, head of the Camp

There were only six of us kept in solitary confinement in camp Me. So everybody knew we were priests. One day, after we had washed bottles of apricot wine during break time, a big young criminal prisoner approached me, asking:

- You're a priest, aren't you?
- Yes, we all are priests.
- How long have you been here?
- Just a few months.
- Do you know the head of camp A?
- I know he is a captain, but I don't know his name.

He then changed his voice, addressing me with reverence:

- Father, I am a Catholic. Mr. H. is my uncle. He and his wife are very religious people. In their room is always hung a picture of the Mother of Perpetual Help. They recite the Rosary every evening before bedtime.

- Why are you detained here?

- I was caught by security officers on a trip to the South to buy religious articles for sale. After confiscating all the items I had bought, they brought me here for disciplinary measures.

- Does you uncle not do anything to help you?

- No problem! I have been caught like this many times before. My uncle just says a few words and everything will be O.K

Break-time was over. I went back to work thinking again and again that now in the North many Catholics were like captain H. They were reluctant to work just for living, or as required by the situation. Any way, those Catholics would be forgiven by God who mercifully looks at their faithful hearts.

The Catholic prisoner did not forget me. He continued to come visiting me once in a while. Before being set free, he also came to say good bye.

November 26, 1997

IX. CAMP THANH CAM
LY BA SO ZONE IV, THANH HOA

We had been used to moving all the time. New hardships were always waiting for us wherever we went. We tried to make friends with cadres on duty and naturally with wardens, asking them to keep us informed of the latest news on where we were going to move. We did not know why the Ministry of the Interior kept changing their mind, now planning to move us up to Camp Cấp Tiến, Cao Bằng, now wanting us to go to Nghệ Tĩnh. Finally, we came to know we had to go to camp Thanh Cẩm, Thanh Hóa. The waiting period lasted a whole month.

The news of our transfer made many anxious, especially the cadres who had got a lot of help from us. The person I missed most was the camp-head. During the long waiting period, he came to see us, almost every day. The rumour about him being a good man was true. What I worried about most was group 20, still being under disciplinary measures. Our absence left a void in their lives. I did not know what to do but to leave them to God and pray for them. Before going, I rushed into the garden near the discipline room and raised my voice, informing them of our departure.

When our journey started, all of the cadres stopped working and ran out to see us off with a vague sadness in their eyes. We only bowed to them in silence. The Molotova carrying us, escorted by a jeep loaded with cadres started to head for Thanh Hoa, about 100 km from Phu Ly. We spent the whole day, covering at least 80km through the woods before reaching camp Thanh Cam.

Camp Thanh Cam is located by the Ma River. It is rather large, but not so large as camp Nam Ha. It appears old, except the main gate, which looks colossal and apparently just rebuilt. As the name of Ly Ba So inspires awe, so does this camp since it is put under the direct control of the security service, notorious for brutality.

After being checked with belongings, we were escorted to a secluded area. At our sight, everyone hurried out to meet us. It turned out that we all were priests and chaplains except some clergymen from the North. We were so happy to see one another. That night, we shared the first dinner in camp. We said grace before eating as we used to do in the seminary. I realized that my fellow priests here were much better informed than I. They continually gave me the latest news of the day. Since my name is "Quế", little wonder I come to be "quê" (rustic), not as "urban" as they are.

At bedtime, our group's leader (Rev. Truong Kim Huong) assigned six of us to six different rooms together with other priests. Cadres came to check our place. Waiting until they shut all the doors and left, we, in each room, began celebrating Mass in secret. I got very emotional at the idea that God loved us so much that he had brought us together after many years of separation. Now, we met alive after having considered each other as dead. (Actually, five chaplains had died in camps). Lying on the bare floor, I could not get to sleep, not because the hard floor was cold, but because so many memories came alive in my mind.

The next morning, not being allowed to open the door, I lay awake, observing around my room. It is about 2m wide, $2^{1/2}$m long and as high as the head of a mid-sized person can reach. The 2-meter width of the room includes 60cm wide passage leading to a relatively clean rest room. Such a small room must however accommodate nine persons altogether. Six of us agreed to lie on the floor, allowing three others of smaller size to occupy the passage.

In the beginning, the policy of solitary confinement was to shut the prisoners in, day and night, not allowing them even to step out into the yard, except to open the door twice a day to take lunch and dinner. In winter, it was fine, but during the hot Summer-days, each room became an oven as doors and window-bars were made of iron. The intense heat lingered till 10:00 p.m. Prisoners could not stand to wear anything but shorts.

Luckily, such a strict policy became loose since the day we came from Nam Ha. Doors were allowed to open early in the morning. We were not confined all day in the room, but allowed to move around within the limit of a secluded area. Therefore, we were able to contact one another more easily. We could cook and eat together. We were also able to receive gifts every month from family visits. All the foods, except medicine, were pooled together for common use. I had the feeling we were living at the time described in the Acts of the Apostles: "Their possessions and goods they sold and divided them to all, according as everyone had need... with glad-ness and simplicity of heart." (2/45, 46)

My old Father's Visit

Since the day feeding visits were allowed, I was not afraid of dying from starvation any more. As priests, we knew for sure that Divine Providence had made it happen not only to save us from death, but also for us to share good things with others and help them comprehend the deep meaning of shar-ing, and go out to share their food with friends in need.

I had been at camp Thanh Cam for almost a week when, one morning the warden came to let me know I had a feeding visit. Who is it, I thought to myself, rather surprised. How come someone knows me here when I have just arrived, without correspondence or connection whatsoever with anybody from the outside world.

I then followed the warden. As soon as I arrived at the reception center, I saw an old man waiting. It is my father. At his sight, I became listless and overcome by emotion. His sudden presence at this place exceeded my expectation. My father came near. We embraced each other, sobbing. He could hardly say: "I try to come here, just to see you with my own eyes for the last time." He then added: "O my God! How come my son happens to be like this." I tried to console him and turned away to shake hands with Hap, my younger brother. He also came here for the first time to see me. We then went into the reception room. The warden said to my father: "Feel free to talk with your son, sir. I will be back at around noon time to take him." My father thanked him and told my brother to give him a pack of cigarettes.

That day, there was nobody in the reception room but us. So we felt very comfortable while talking with each other. I asked my father:

- Why do you know I am here, Dad?

- I was told you were in camp Phủ Lý. It is accessible by car, so I told your brother Hap to take me there to see you. At my age, 87, I really want to see you by all means before I die, which can happen anytime according to God's will. However, I arrived there only to find that you had been transferred elsewhere. Feeling sorry for my old age, a cadre by the name I don't remember exactly Cao or Rao said a few comforting words and then let me know you had been transferred to camp Thanh Cam here. I know the journey to Thanh Hoa is long and full of hurdles. Still, I was determined to go and told your brother Hap to take me there to look for you.

Actually, my father just arrived yesterday afternoon. So he was still very tired. I sat close to him, putting my arm around his shoulder and trying to stop him. Before I could ask him about the family situation, he continued:

- When reaching Thanh Hoa, your brother and I had to ask several times for direction to camp Thanh Cam. We finally found out that the way to the camp was 80km long, running through forests and over brooks. As for transportation, people told us that it was too late for the bus, and that if we wanted to walk, we could do so, hopefully to find a horse or buffalo-drawn cart on the way to share the ride. In such a situation, we did not know what to do, but to take risks. We started the journey, me on a walking stick, your brother carrying a heavy load of over 100kg of food. After walking about 100 meters, I collapsed on the road from exhaustion. Fearing that I could possibly die along the way, your brother proposed to return to Thanh Hoa for a future plan. Luckily, at that time, a military Molotova happened to pass by. When they saw an old man lying on the road, they stopped to ask what had happened. We told them our problem, begging for help. Feeling sorry for an old man, they said: "We go the same direction. We can give you a lift if you don't mind waiting as we have to stop once in a while for some errands."

He then helped me into the car and drove away. The car traveled at high speed on a rough road weaving its way through the woods, causing my side to bleed against the body of the car. I still feel the pain now. When we arrived here, I told your brother to give them some tip money and a pack of cigarettes. I am so thankful to God and Mother Mary for a safe journey. And now, I am so happy to see you here.

The story of my father's trip touched my heart very deeply. It reflects an intense love he has for me and revives in me the indomitable spirit of my ancestors. One of them is Saint martyr Dinh Viet Du whom my dear mother has taught me to honor and pray for protection since my childhood till now. I asked my father about everything: family, relatives, friends, my Congregation and even about the world and Vietnam situation after the day of "liberation". Also, I would like him to convey my regards to relatives and friends living abroad. I carefully recommended that my younger brother should take care of my parents during my absence, especially in case

I die in prison, and replace me to see about the funeral service of my parents when they pass away. To my belief, God has planned this meeting so that my father and I can encourage and comfort each other for the last time.

At noon, my brother prepared lunch for us. We were eating when the warden appeared. He told us to go ahead with our meal. My brother offered him a cigarette. He smoked and sat down to talk with my father. I have to admit that my father is very clever at establishing friendly relations with others, thus winning him respect from everyone. Gifted with the skill of a diplomat, he has been able to overcome so many hurdles on the way to the camp.

At 2:00 p.m. the cadre ordered me to return to camp. I gave my father a final embrace before leaving. My brother carried the food to the camp gate for me. When I turned back, I saw my father still standing there looking at me. I waved him good bye before stepping into the gate.

Never in my life can I forget all the hardships you had suffered when you came to the camp to see me, Dad!

Family Affairs

After being released in 1988, I came home to fulfill my filial duties till the beginning of 1993 when my conscience as of a priest dictated me to leave my old parents for the United States. My father willingly let me go in peace because he had dedicated

228

his son to God. Though in the United States, thousands of miles away, I tried to make my father feel that I was not far from him by continually sending him letters, gifts, even inquiring after his health on phone.

My stepmother's Death

My stepmother died on Sept, 11th, 93. Unable to go home, I asked Nguyen Thi Mai, my younger brother's wife to go and represent us and the whole family to attend the funeral service. As my father wished to die first, so did my mother. Now that she had satisfied her wish. In the United States, as sons, nephews and nieces, we gathered at the Blessed Sacrament Church in Westminster to mourn her and celebrate a Requiem Mass for the soul of Mary. May she soon enjoy God's presence in Heaven.

My Father's Death

With only a father still on earth, my brothers and I took turns going home to see him, not to mention the fact that we had to supply for his material needs, especially in the later years, we found that our father's health was noticeably deteriorating. He appeared very happy at the news that his youngest son Dinh Quang Truat would go home to see him during the summer of 1996. But God had planned for him otherwise. In the middle of March, 1996, he seemed very exhausted. Knowing that my brothers at home intended to inform me of the bad news, he stopped them, saying; "No, don't make him worry or distract his mind! Let him concentrate on his pastoral duties for the glory of God!" Truly, as a pastor in charge of a rather large Catholic Community, I was very busy especially during the Lent season. My father might know that, and he wanted to offer his son as the ultimate sacrifice to God. Furthermore, out of great devotion to Mary, he prayed that he could die on a Saturday. He spent days and nights, reciting the Rosary and praying for those he knew, especially for the souls still in the purgatory. My father's prayers had been answered. He died on Saturday preceding Palm Sunday, March 30, 1996.

Peter Dinh Van Phac has come home to his Heavenly Father

(A notice from the Congregation of the Redemptorists, Saigon)

Rev. Dinh Ngoc Que's father, Senior Peter Dinh Van Phac has come home to his Heavenly Father on Saturday before Palm Sunday, March 30, 1996 at Bui Chu parish, Ho Nai, Bien Hoa at the age of 96.

The following morning, March 31, 1996, Rev. Dinh Ngoc Que and two of his younger brothers: Dinh Ngoc Thu and Dinh Ngoc Truat arrived home from California to attend their father's funeral as dutiful sons.

The 8:00 a.m. funeral mass was celebrated at Bui Chu Church on Holiday Wednesday, April 4, 1996 by Rev. Dinh Ngoc Que, together with 53 concelebrants including seculars and regulars as well, and with the participation of a great number of parishioners, brothers and sisters from various religious orders, and organizations. Also present at the funeral were Provincial Superior Cao Dinh Tri and his delegate, Rev. Tran Ngoc Thao, director of the learning Institute, Rev. Pham Gia Thuy novice master, Rev. Nguyen Huu Phu, father superior of Mai Thon, Rev. Nguyen Tu Do, father fuperior of Clement congregation, together with brothers of the Congregation amounting to 60 persons. All of them had come by bus to Ho Nai since early morning.

Through records of his life confirmed by the pastor of Bui Chu parish in his sermon, we came to know that Senior Phac was a faithful son of God, passionately devoted to the Holy Church's development. Not to mention some of his children and grandchildren called to religious life for God's service, he himself had served as a head of the third Dominican Order, a parish Council member for many years and as a foreman for the church construction. After the Mass, Rev. Cao Dinh Tri presided over the funeral ceremony. He was buried at the cemetery of Bui Chu parish. May he share the glory of Easter following the Holy Week commemorating Jesus' death on the Cross.

Rev. Dinh Ngoc Que remained in Vietnam for two more weeks after his father had been laid to rest. He returned to Saigon monastery to celebrate Easter with his fellow Redemptorists. Together with a delegation of about 100 persons headed by Rev. Nguyen Tu Do, he spent the Holy Saturday, visiting and donating gifts to the lepers at Ben San camp, and also celebrating Pass-over Mass at a chapel where three lepers were baptized and received the sacrament of confirmation that very night.

The 40th Anniversary
of ordination to the Priesthood

When my father's burial service was done, I stayed at 38 Ky Dong St., Saigon. During that time, I and three of my classmates: Rev. Dinh Khac Trieu, Rev. Nguyen Van Phu, Rev. Nguyen Tu Do (except Rev. Tran Dinh Phuc and Rev. Nguyen Van Thong still in the United States), we gathered to celebrate our 40th anniversary of ordination to the priesthood.

The concelebration of Mass was held at the parish of the Mother of Perpetual Help's church, with the full participation of secular and regular priests, and their family members, brothers and sisters from various congregations and organizations, especially Curia members of the Mother of Perpetual Help, Parish council's members and Parishioners. Rev. Dinh Khac Trieu, the oldest in our group was the Mass main celebrant and sermon deliverer. Following the Mass, Rev. Cao Dinh Tri, the Provincial Superior, in a short speech, applauded us for having made a significant contribution to the service of the Congregation and the faithful. He wished that we would continue our good work for the glory of God and for the salvation of the souls.

The Mass was followed by a reception party in the Hiep Nhat park of the parish. Invited guests were over 600 people. Everybody present felt very happy. It was an event I can never forget, especially after my father's death.

I am thankful to God that he has bestowed on me so many blessings through long years of my priesthood, serving as a teacher, a missionary, an army chaplain and a prisoner until today. I am grateful to my parents, my benefactors and all others for having helped me to the sacred altar in one way or another. Everyday, I celebrate the Holy Mass to praise God and pray for them.

The situation of a number of priests in prison

In solitary confinement at Camp Thanh Cam, we were able to breathe a little bit more easily, anyway. Though not allowed to contact other prisoners, even cadres, we were however able to talk with other priests in neighboring rooms. As a result, I came to know the real condition of some priests in prison. Following are some typical cases:

Rev. Nguyen Huu Le's escape

Rev. Nguyen Huu Le is not an army chaplain. He was captured while trying to flee the country. He was taken to the North and put in prison together with political prisoners. Rev. Le had tried to escape with former colonel Trinh Tien and major

Tiep a couple of years before I came to camp Thanh Cam, here. It was not long however before they were caught back. Colonel Tien was the first to be recaptured. They gathered to beat him to death and dumped his body into a discipline room. Rev. Nguyen Huu Le was caught second. They beat him brutally until he fainted. Thinking he was dead, they dragged his body to the room where colonel Tien's corpse was lying and threw him over it. Finally, major Tiep was caught and beaten to death. His body was carried to the same room to be put together with two others. After that, they locked the door, leaving three bodies behind.

During the night when the heat softened, Rev. Le recovered consciousness and found that he was lying on Mr. Tien's corpse, and above him, Mr. Tiep was dying. He still felt very painful and too weak to move. He had to stay put, trying to help Mr. Tiep die a peaceful death in God.

The next morning, cadres came and found Rev. Le was still alive. They then locked his hands and feet in stocks and confined him in another room. After that, they made report about the death of the two prisoners before burying them. At the beginning, Rev. Le was put in hand and foot stocks continually for an entire month. Afterwards, he was only in foot-stocks during the night, and was disciplined for more than two years. We had been in solitary confinement several months before he was allowed to come and live with us. He looked so thin and pale with cuts and bruises caused by repeated beating still all over his body. A lot of antibiotic was required to alleviate the trauma and headache he was suffering. A bear's gallbladder was particularly needed to soften the pain caused by cuts and bruises. Rev. Le was released one year after me (in 1989). He stayed in Saigon only for a short period of time before successfully fleeing the country. He is now in New Zealand, serving as a pastor for a Catholic Community. He has been to the United States twice. We were so happy to meet, Thank God!

Rev. Hung with a foot amputated

Before 1975, Rev. Hung had served as a chaplain for Gia Dinh sub-zone under the control of the Capital Special Zone. He had been taken to the North and kept in solitary confinement at Thanh Cam several years before I came. At that time, the confinement regulations were very strict. No feeding visits, no contacts whatsoever with the outside world. Prisoners were shut off in their rooms. Bath was allowed only once a month. They were left in extremely dirty conditions, suffering from permanent hunger and malnutrition. He was for unknown reason disciplined with feet locked in stocks. When released from the stocks, one of his feet got badly hurt from friction against the grip of the stocks on his ankles. For lack of iodine and antibiotic, the wound did not heal and became worse with microphage-infection, causing him a great deal of pain. Not allowed to be in the infirmary, he was forced to remain in bed, moaning and groaning all night, keeping others awake. In such a circumstance, the warden had to put him in a discipline room far away. One day, while checking around the discipline area, a cadre on duty happened to see him. Surprised at his presence there (because he was not among the disciplined) the cadre asked the reason and came to understand his pitiful situation. He then promised to help.

A few days later, thanks to the cadre's intervention, Rev. hung was given medical attention in the infirmary. It was too late, alas! The microphages had eaten away into his bone. His foot was becoming so badly damaged that physicians had to amputate it, above the ankles to save his life.

By the time I came to the camp and shared the room with Rev.Hung, his amputated leg had been healed, and he had to walk on crutches. Feeling sorry for his debilitating condition, I gave him a tael of tiger-bone jelly for recuperation.

I really admire Rev. Hung for his strong will and faith life. After living in the United States for a few years, I sent him some gifts only to find out that he had passed away. Rev. Hung had given all his life to the service of God and other people. He had really died a heroic death. May God receive his self-immolation and give him an eternal life.

Treatment of scabies
for Rev. Nguyen Thien Thuat and Rev. Hoa

Rev. Thuat used to serve as a chaplain for the navy staff under the control of the Capital Special Zone. Rev. Hoa nicknamed "foreman" was a secular priest of the diocese of Binh Duong. He was not a chaplain. Both were kept in solitary confinement. They were infected with scabies due to malnutrition and unsanitary conditions. Their bodies were crawling with mangy pustules, exuding a putrid and nauseating odor.

Until now, I just cannot imagine how much civilized the Communists thought they were when they ordered father Thuat and father Hoa, together with other prisoners infected with scabies to take off clothes and stand totally naked in the ground and sprayed all over them with a container of DDT (a kind of pesticide). When the spraying was done, they let them go. I asked both of them: "How is your scabies?" Not answering my question, they just said: "It's so embarrassing!"

Later on, after they had been fed by family visits, all forms of mange were gone. Rev. Thuat looked younger. Rev. Hoa, who used to have a dark complexion just like a cement mason's (that's why we called him a foreman) looked more handsome with clear skin.

After the release, we met again in Saigon. Each time, we met them, we usually asked them jokingly: "How is your scabies?" They just blushed while we were laughing heartily. It was so much fun to recall the memories we had shared together in prison.

Rev. Dinh Cao Thuan and the picture of St. Mary

As a head of the Catholic chaplain Directorate, Rev. Dinh Cao Thuan had appointed me to be a chaplain. I had a chance to meet him again at the secluded area in Camp Thanh Cam. As a person with many skills, he spent his spare time playing guitar, writing poems or drawing pictures. He said to me: "They are easy now. They used to check on everything we did before. About a year ago, I was disciplined for several months just because a cadre discovered a picture of Mary I drew, hidden under a pillow. He then put me in solitary confinement, on the charge that I was spreading faith. Now we can breathe easier because this "Vatican" zone (as they often call it, meaning that the priests are fed by Vatican) has helped them satisfy some of their material needs. Now, they understand the priests very well and do not consider us as CIA any more."

In 1988, Rev. Dinh Cao Thuan was set free together with me. And together, we remained in the North for one month before returning to the South. We took time visiting various places in Bui Chu, our hometown and celebrating the Tet festival with my relatives and friends. Now, Rev. Dinh cao Thuan is serving as the pastor of Xay Dung parish at Ong Ta crossroads.

No more Youth time for Rev. D.T.T

Most of us, priests, were arrested and imprisoned at the age when we were active. Some, younger, at around 30, were still in their prime. They were just ordained to the priesthood a few years ago. They had been promised only one month of reeducation, whereas years and years had passed without any hope of being released. Isolated in the dense woods for more than a decade without any chance of learning to improve their knowledge besides bitter experiences in prison, they suffered a great deal from the feeling that their youth time had been wasted unreasonably.

Since the day I came here, we concelebrated Mass in secret everyday. One day, during the Mass, a young priest when sharing the God's words complained: "O Lord! If you let me stay on and on at this place, my young age is certainly lost..." He sobbed bitterly, unable to say further. My heart sank when I thought of the young priest's complaints. I could not get to sleep that night, thinking of my own situation, not very much different from his. I, too had a lot to lose. I was often complaining: "How can I live, O Lord!"

The next day, on the way to the labor field, I happened to stand in line with the young priest who had complained about his fate during the Mass the day before. When we were out of the gate, I asked him: "Did you say yesterday that you had lost your young age, didn't you? Why are you so pessimistic?"

239

Unexpectedly hurt by my remark, he pointed his hand to my face, saying bluntly: "Don't you know, as a chaplain for a long time, you have enjoyed a lot of things: money, name, power, many amenities of life and everything. As for me, I have got nothing before being captured, and now I am living a miserable life year after year, deprived of any hope. Don't you think that my young age is lost? Why are you so insensitive to my suffering?" Really, I was not delicate when reminding him of all his misfortunes. What he said, was true. He had no time to enjoy anything before being arrested. Yes, his young age had been being lost. Since then, I always remember him in my prayers, and we have become close friends.

Right now, he is in charge of a poor parish in a secluded village in the Far West of Vietnam. I feel much grief and regret at the idea that the revolution has been destroying so many skills and talents, so many young people and so many best brains of the country. What a waste of human resources! Is that what the Revolution for? It's a heart-wrenching question nobody can ever answer.

O Lord! Only you can save our miserable country.

Premonitory brutal beatings
Any time, anywhere, the words "public security" always inspire awe. To them, human life is so cheap!

I'm gonna ask you for a tooth

In the secluded area, every four rooms shared a yard separated by a wall. Prisoners could not see their friends in other rooms, but they were able to hear someone talk loudly in another room easily. Standing on the window sill however, they could look down the yard of another room and see what was happening there. One evening, I saw a cadre bring a number of criminal prisoners to a room next to mine. The cadre locked the door, ready to go. At that time, I heard a criminal prisoner cursing something in a loud voice, meaning that he did not care a damn about the cadre. Unluckily for him, the cadre did not go far enough. Hearing the curse, he came back, and asked angrily: "Who just cursed me?" Nobody dared to say a word. Unable to get somebody to admit guilt, the cadre became more upset, threatening to put the whole group under discipline. Finally, someone in the group offered to denounce the culprit. The cadre then shouted at him: "It's you, right? Tomorrow morning when you go for labor, I'm gonna ask you for a tooth. You hear me?" Upon those threatening words, he left.

From my room, I noticed everything, wondering if he really meant business or it was just a warning. After the cadre's departure,when everything came back to normal, we started to concelebrate Mass in secret in our room.

The next morning, when the time to go for hard labor came, I saw two cadres, a heavy padlock in hands, hasten to the nearby room, unlock the door and pull out the prisoner who had cursed the day before. They forcibly pushed him into the yard, saying: "We're gonna let you know who we really are." Once in the yard, he was repeatedly and brutally attacked with heavy padlocks right on the head until he fainted and collapsed on the ground, face smashed with blood, with two front-teeth broken. Very satisfied with their "feat", they had the victim carried into a room, saying: "A lesson for him to remember forever."

Some of my fellow priests and I, we were really frightened while secretly observing such a horrible scene from the window. I asked myself: "Who has given them the right to treat a human being like that. Really, man is more than wolf to man."

Because of a sugar cane

We suffered from permanent hunger in camp. Criminal prisoners however suffered more than we did. Adding to the miseries was the fact that prisoners turned out to be the victims of "voracious bears" who often appropriated the best parts of the gifts received from families. Otherwise, they were beaten brutally. One day, at the reception center, I happened to see a scene which could break my heart. A countrywoman in tatters came to visit her imprisoned son. At the sight of his mother, the son did not say a word. He just asked his mother bluntly: "Where are my gifts?" The mother silently handed her son a

242

small box containing only some handfuls of rice, a few dried fish, a little bit of salt with sesame seeds and a couple of bananas. He sat right down on the ground and kept eating until he was full, not aware of his mother who was watching in tears.

Back to camp, I kept wondering about the way the son had treated his poor mother. Later, when asking one of my fellow priests for the reason, I came to know that every prisoner had to act like that, otherwise most of their gifts would be eaten away by "voracious bears." What a pity for the mother and for the son, too!

It is the hunger that engenders so much trouble.

Cadres' common practice was to bring prisoners home and used them as domestics for their private purposes such as washing, cleaning, sweeping, carrying water, gardening, planting... under their wives' supervision.

The prisoners were allowed back to camp when they finished their assigned work for the day. They might be given something to eat in case they got the job done satisfactorily.

One day, while weeding around some sugar canes at a cadre's house, a criminal prisoner stealthily cut off one of them to quench his thirst. Unluckily, he was caught in the act by the cadre's wife who just came home from market. She showered curses on him and angrily told him that she would inform her husband.

That very evening when all prisoners had been

back to camp, the cadre had the culprit reported in the yard. No sooner had the prisoner arrived than the cadre suddenly struck him twice on the shin with a carrying pole. The prisoner screamed with pain before collapsing, unconscious.

I happened to see such a terrible scene from the window of my room. Yes, a sugar cane might be of some value to him. He could sell it for a few cents to buy some rice for his poor family. But I was not able to comprehend why the prisoner was treated so brutally after he had served that family faithfully for several months. To me, being inhuman like that is much worse than stealing something just because of hunger.

Living conditions of Cadres and their families

While traveling from camp to camp in the North, I found that people in general were very poor. Even young cadres were also from poor families, most of them illiterate, but very haughty and arrogant. A majority of young men were killed during the war, leaving the hard work of farming to women. As a result, children left home early, living a life of debauchery for lack of parental guidance and formal education.

Not even a word of Thanks was ever heard in daily life

As a principal of five schools in Saigon with a number of students totaling at least 2000, and as a chaplain for various organizations: Gia Long school-girls, Capital scouts, Hung Tam Dung Chi movements... I used to have a special affection for the young generation. When in prison, I was still strongly attached to young people. I felt very happy to meet young cadres. I liked to help them insofar as I could. Therefore, they often came to talk with me.

One day, an armed cadre I had known for long, came to tell me about his love story. I took that opportunity to explain to him the true meaning of love and marriage happiness. Enthralled by my explanations, he showed me the portrait of his love, and asked for advice. He seemed to put all trust in me.

Cadres' children often came to play in the camp-ground while we were working. I secretly gave them some candies. To them, candies made in Saigon were much better than those made in the North. Hair-cutting was not my trade, but I did it rather well. So cadres often came to me for a hair-cut. Each time, I got it done, they stood up, saying okay with a haughty attitude. To my remembrance, I never heard a word of thanks from the cadres as well as from the children after I had given them some help. I might say the word of thanks had almost been excluded from the Northern language. Therefore, I thought, how can they thank their parents, their benefactors and finally how can they be thankful to God? Our ancestors were certainly right when they placed moral education above literary instruction.

Conjugal Fidelity is insignificant

Following is the story recounted by a political prisoner who served as a domestic for a cadre's family.

One day, when visiting his friend, a cadre informed him of his wife's infidelity. The host just answered his guest with a shrug, saying: "My wife is still strong and healthy. Let her do it as she wishes. I don't care." Such an indifferent attitude indicates that marriage does not mean anything, and the "Live and Let Live" policy prevails in family life now.

In my camp, there was a criminal prisoner being caught red-handed with his wife for smuggling goods. Thanks to some form of bribery, only he was arrested and imprisoned. A month later, his wife came to visit him, with a letter saying that her visit was the first and also the last one. She then asked him to sign on the divorce paper, so that she would be allowed to marry another man, just because she could not wait any longer. Forced to sign, he was suddenly thrown into a state of mind nobody could understand but himself.

Is that marriage all about? Certainly not. Marriage is not a deal to make. It is a commitment to honor throughout one's life. Marriage happiness involves sorrows and joys to share. True love requires fidelity. No wonder, those who treat marriage as of little importance, get divorced easily.

Going for Hard labor

Labor is hard, indeed; but psychologically speaking, it's still better than just sitting there in a walled-in prison, doing nothing, which might easily send you to the mental hospital.

I had been in camp Thanh Cam for nearly one year, doing nothing but eating, sleeping, sitting in one place day and night. Never in my life had I felt so bored. When asking for something to do, we got an ambigous answer from the warden: "The staff has not been able to make any arrangement yet."

Our desire was satisfied at last. They allowed us to work within the camp limits.

First of all, our job was to weave lattices in the campground. Criminal prisoners went into the jungle to cut "nua" (one of the bamboo family with a hollow stem) and piled them up at the corner of the campground, ready for us. We smashed their stems in tapes to weave lattices 2^m30 long and 1^m wide. The norm for each person to achieve was 10 lattices a day. We worked in groups, adopting the system of assembly line. We were praised for high achievements, thus generating income to the camp.

Realizing that we, as priests, were conscientious workers, especially our work turned out to be very fruitful, they devised more projects for us to carry out: weaving hats and baskets for sale. Any article we produced, was cleverly made, beautiful-looking and of good lasting quality, beyond their expectations.

The weaving period lasted for about one year before construction need arose. Criminal prisoners were forced to mine mountains for rocks. The rocks were then carried down to the campground for us to break into small stones for concrete. The process required a lot of effort and muscle. Some of young priests struck big rocks with a heavy hammer for smaller fragments, the size of a road-paving stones, while others hammered these stones by driving nails into them for even smaller ones, ready for making concrete.

The job of hammering rocks all day long appeared to be easy, but actually it was very risky with debris shooting all around, sometimes breaking our looking glasses, or flying right into our eyes. If we were not careful, the hammer might strike our fingers, causing serious bleeding. The daily norm for each of us was one basket full of rocks, heavy enough for two persons to carry and submit to the cadres.

Since the day we were allowed to work in the campground, I had the opportunity to contact a number of criminal prisoners and political ones from the South. I found that the criminal prisoners were living in hellish conditions. They were destitute, I might say, and permanently hungry. They usually turned to political prisoners for help.

As for political prisoners, they were seemingly neither interested in one another, nor enthusiastic about community activities, for lack of leadership. There were 40 priests in the camp, but they were all confined in solitary, with no communication whatsoever with the outside world. Tet festival was the only occasion for them to meet others.

The number of political prisoners was about 600 or 700, including quite a few Catholics. On holidays, I often signaled them to get ready for receiving the sacrament of reconciliation in public. When there was no Mass, I secretly handed consecrated bread to a representative for distribution. We were permanently kept informed of the situation of friends "down there" through those who came up to gather human waste behind our secluded area.

A Big Project: Tea plantation

One day, a central delegation accompanied by two lieutenant colonels and a great number of khaki-uniformed cadres came to visit our camp. When arriving at the place where we were breaking rocks, they inquired about our situation and praised us for high standard of production.After making a tour around the camp, they left.

The following day, we had an order to stop working on the rocks and get ready for another job. What kind of job, I wondered. It finally turned out to be a tea plantation. I heard about it long time ago, but we had to wait until the central delegation came to make a final decision. Since we were allowed to work together with the rest of the camp, and outside the camp, we were certainly going to meet a new challenge, but have more fun while in contact more often with other political prisoners.

Camp Thanh Cam was by the Ma river, with numerous bare hills to the Northeast, about a kilo-meter away. Camp authorities targeted those hills for tea growing. We worked together in a group. Still considering us as elements of solitary confine-ment, they kept a closer watch over us. But in reality, everyone worked the same in the field.

The first thing for us to do was to clean up the hills. Small or large, all kinds of trees must be felled and uprooted. My group was assigned to dig up the stumps. The norm for each person was to have three stumps (one large and two small) removed a day. Working tools were one cleaver for each person, one crow bar, one shovel and one ax for common use. We broke into groups of three and worked in the spirit of mutual help. We found the job very hard at first, causing too much strain to our hands. We tried to learn from experience and gradually came up to a high standard of achievement, for which we were given a public commendation in the campground.

It took all the groups half a year to work hard to get the cleaning of hills done. Then came the sec-ond phase, weeding and bedding. After bedding, we did the sowing and watering. We formed two groups, one for weeding, and another for bedding. When it came to sowing, only a few specialists were in charge while the rest of us took turns to carry water and do the watering. The watering task consumed a lot of sweat. We had to walk down to the Ma river, at least half a kilometer away, to get water, and then to carry it uphill to the top, or sometimes over to the other side of the hill. The distant scene of so many people weaving their way uphill with buckets of water on their shoulders resembled a long line of ants carrying food up the mountain. To the outsiders, the sight looked very nice, but to us, the insiders, it was so time-consuming and exhausting to carry water uphill and water all over the hill. When we suggested the idea of watering by machine for shorter time and convenience, their answer was: "No money."

During the dry season, the watering job got even harder. We could not afford enough water for so many tea plantations on the hills, leaving at least two percent of tea plants go dry and wither before they could get water. Camp authorities knew that, however they did nothing but count on our labor, as they often said: "Water of the river, but labor of the prisoners." We knew that, too. But as prisoners, we could not do otherwise. It was said later that the project of growing tea was left unfinished due to lack of fund and human labor.

To grow peanuts for oil
Since the camp authorities could not afford to go on with the tea-growing project, they ordered us to grow peanuts for oil. In the middle of the river emerges a rather large island, about one-kilometer away from the camp. When the water subsides, the island can be reached by wading. They targeted the

251

island for growing peanuts. Therefore we had to wade there everyday for the job. Tractors did the cleaning. Our job was to cultivate the soil and do the bedding, which was relatively easy. The best part of the job was for me to have a chance to go over to other groups of political prisoners for conversation, thus understanding them better and attending to their material and spiritual needs.

Personality of a priest

The visitation of friends was fun, but it involved risks and caused a lot of headache. While working in the island, we usually had lunch right in the labor field. I took advantage of the break time when the cadres gathered to have lunch, to make connections with other groups. One day, when going back to my group to work again, I happened to pass by the area where cadres were eating. At my sight, one of them asked me to wash dishes for him. As a straight person, I never attempted to win anybody's favor by servile behavior, especially in that situation, to fawn on a cadre, which would cause people to misunderstand that I had a weak personality. Thinking so, I refused his request on the grounds that I had to go back to my group to work in time. He shouted at me, blaming me for lying, but I kept going without turning back, thinking to myself that my duty was to go back to my group to work, not to serve anybody at that time; and I did not mind the consequence of my courageous behavior. Nothing happened since that time, Thank God!

One other day, when a cadre requested me to do the laundry for him, I acted the same way simply to be reproached, and all those hassles came to nothing.

Another time, on the way back to camp, an armed guard with a rifle on shoulder was pushing a bicycle along. He turned to me walking beside him, ordering:

- Mr. Que, take care of this bicycle for me!

- I don't know how to push a bicycle, sir. I replied.

- Don't you really know how to push a bicycle? Why? He showed anger in his voice.

- Really, I don't know. By the way, I don't want to take a risk. I may break your bicycle, sir.

While he was still in hesitation, not knowing what to say, a friend of mine (Father T.Q.T) silenced him by adding: "Mr. Que is right, sir!" Really, he doesn't know how to handle a bicycle. He used to handle only a four-tyred bicycle (meaning a car). Please, try to understand him, sir!" I turned to my fellow priest with a grateful look. We arrived at the camp with no further trouble, that day. Thank God!

A garden of green vegetables

We did not have to go far for work any more. Now, our group was assigned to do the gardening right at the riverside near the main gate of the camp. Horticulture was what I had done before with some experience, so I liked it. We did the digging, weeding, bedding, fertilizing before growing various kinds of vegetables, especially white radish, head-cabbage, bok-choy, "Bách Thảo" (Chinese one-hundred-leaf vegetable).

With all the weeds removed, the garden looked neat, clean and very well-cultivated. While gardening, the task of watering seemed the hardest. We took turns to carry water from the Ma River for watering the garden. Unable to carry water due to the great pain I suffered in the shoulders, I was forced to water vegetables with both hands. The volume of water I used a day for watering might amount to 100 bucketfuls, which put a great strain on my arms.

When it comes to gardening, it is commonly said, water first, fertilizer second, industriousness third and seeds fourth. Seeds were always available either from the camp's supply or from our families' contribution. Nobody could equal us, as priests, in industriousness. As for fertilizer, gardening needed human waste, cow manure and livestock waste. Chemical fertilizer was used particularly for green vegetables. But this kind of fertilizer was always in short supply because it was partly appropriated by cadres, partly stolen by criminal prisoners. Therefore, the big job for us was to water the garden as much as possible. We tried to focus all our efforts on this job. My technique was to encourage the vegetables to grow while watering, by saying: "Come on, dear! Grow up! Grow up fast!" As if to respond to my encouraging words, they started growing so fast that the news reached the government authorities. They sent a central delegation to the camp for inspection. They had to admit that going from Hanoi to Thanh Hoa and from Thanh Hoa to Thanh Cam, they had not seen any farm better than this one, achieved by the priest prisoners. It looked so green and clean, graced with bok choys having elongated leaves reaching up to one meter, and head cabbages sometimes as heavy as 3 or 4 kilograms. The cadres who wanted to enjoy the fresh produce of good quality from our farm, often had to deal privately with the warden for it.

We were happy with the result of our labor, thinking that we had been able to supply fresh vegetables for the whole camp.

Love from God's children
The place where priests were confined, were dubbed "Vatican Zone" by the cadres. Living there, we sought secret ways to attend to various needs of many prisoners, especially to the spiritual needs of the Catholics, even though we were not able to achieve results as good as in camp Nam Ha.

We focused our special attention on the cadres, trying to make them understand us by showing we loved them and cared about them. Even the head of the camp turned to me for medicine for his sick child. Cadres also came to me for thread and needles for their needlework etc.

A sewing needle

One day, while checking a box of gifts I had just received, a cadre found in it some needles and a roll of yarn. He waited until bedtime and came to me to borrow needles and yarn for sewing. I handed him the whole bunch of them. I waited and waited the entire month, and he did not return what he had borrowed. When I met him in the labor field and reminded him of my sewing box, he promised to give it back. That night, he came to my room to return two needles and the remaining yarn. Feeling sorry for him, I gave him one needle in silence. With a happy look on his face, he said: "Your needle is excellent. Needles made in socialist countries break easily." When he left, I felt very sorry for him, at the idea that such a small thing as a simple needle could make him happy, which indicated that he and his family were still in need of many other things. In the North, secluded from the civilized world, the supply of good products was very limited.

A Seminary in Miniature

Confined in solitary at camp Thanh Cam were 39 priests and one seminarist. Most of them were former chaplains from the South. The remaining six priests ordained in secret and one seminarist were from dioceses of Bui Chu, Phat Diem, Bac ninh and Hai Phong. Of six priests ordained in secret, father T. from Bui Chu is worth mentioning. As a seminarist, he was arrested twice and sentenced to

14 years of reeducation. Once secretly ordained to the priesthood, he was sentenced again to 6 more years. He spent 20 years in all in reeducation camps just for embracing a religious life. He was confined together with us for the last several months.

One day, while walking along with me to the labor field, a priest (named N.) from the diocese of Bui Chu asked me to help him improve his knowledge of the Bible, so that after being released he would be able to perform his pastoral duties more effectively. I agreed to help him. But, on the way back to camp, I though to myself: How about other priests and a seminarist from the North? Why not help them at the same time for convenience as long as we're still living together. Furthermore, present here are quite a few priests from the South who have been graduated from various schools of theology. They are certainly capable of helping them in many other subjects concerning theology, besides the Bible.

The next morning, on the way to labor, I met Rev. N. and let him know my idea. He then went back to his colleagues. All of them happily agreed with me about the project.

The plan was scheduled to start in about a week. Everything must be kept secret, otherwise I could be in big trouble, if not be put in stocks. I began to contact Southern priests and discussed with them about the program. They were all willing to help. While teaching, we did not go into details. Rather, we stressed the importance of the method of learning and research.

Following subjects were included in the program:

· Bible: the Old and New Testaments (presented by Rev. T.V.T)

· Theology: God's salvation plan (presented by Rev. D.N.Q)

· The Redeemer: His life and activities; his death and Resurrection. (presented by Rev. D.N.Q)

· The Holy Church: The mystery of Christ (presented by Rev. H.)

· Philosophy: scholastic and Oriental (presented by Rev. D.C.T)

· Existentialism (presented by Rev. H.H)

· Liturgy: The Eucharist; God's words (in case of absence of priests) (presented by Rev. D.N.Q)

· Sacred Music (presented by Rev. N.V.M)

· Pastoral duties: Preparations for Marriage and family life. (presented by Rev. D.N.Q)

I served as a liaison and co-ordinator of the program. Daily classes started after labor. There were morning classes and afternoon classes on Sundays and Holidays. We always had someone watch out for sudden appearance of cadres.

After a whole week preparations, we, including me with seven other priests and one seminarist from the North, concelebrated Mass for opening classes which lasted for more than three months. I really admired their studiousness and endeavor in gaining knowledge. Their humble lives brought down from

Heaven a lot of blessings upon them, enabling them to fulfill their pastoral duties.

As we often sent letters home in secret, so the priests from the North wrote to their respective bishops, telling about my initiative in camp. They got an answer from the bishop of Phat Diem, saying: "Though in prison, you are luckier than we are at home. My regards and many thanks to Rev. Que and his colleagues for their wonderful idea."

By the end of the third month, we knew by hearsay that the priests from the North would be released from solitary confinement and allowed to go "down there" to live with political prisoners. At the news, I told the priests in charge to summarize their text in order to terminate the program sooner.

We marked the close of the program with a Thanksgiving Mass and a farewell meal.

When they left, I encouraged them to learn more foreign languages such as English and French so that they might enrich their knowledge in many other fields. I also tried to contact former professors of the university of Saigon asking to help them. I felt very happy at the idea that I had succeeded in doing something good for the future of the Church of Vietnam and in realizing right in camp the solidarity between us, priests, and those who had dedicated their lives to God.

A Public security agent who wanted to convert to Catholicism

It is my habit to exercise daily to stay healthy. I can exercise anywhere, at home, in prison and now in the United States. Only when we are sick can we realize the importance of good health. Only when in prison, exhausted from starvation, lack of sleep, hard labor, can we experience the need of physical strength and especially of the power of mind. Deprived of those two kinds of strength, we find it very hard to stay alive. Therefore, I try to set a good example to others.

One Sunday morning, while exercising in the nearby ground, I was startled by a sudden call from behind: "Hey! Hey! mister!" I turned back and saw a criminal prisoner standing against the window-bars. He seemingly wanted to tell me something. My natural reaction was to keep silence before a stranger, especially when he was a newcomer and when I did not know for sure what kind of person he was. Furthermore, as a prisoner in solitary confinement, I was forbidden to talk with the outsiders. So, I only waved to him and went back to my room. The following Sunday, also the Holiday of the camp when our area became deserted and cadres were not around, I entered the nearby ground for a work-out, and at the same time, to find out further about the newcomer. As I had expected, when my work-out was over, the stranger appeared. He called me, wanting to talk with me. Looking around to make sure there were nobody present, I approached the window of his room and asked: "What do you want?" He answered: "I just wonder why you, a priest, look so happy while in prison." At such a sudden question, I could not respond the way I wished. I just pointed to my breast, saying: "We're happy thanks to this." (meaning thanks to God's love in my heart.) But I was pretty sure he did not see my point. I then changed the subject, and inquired about him:

- How long have you been here? Why are you arrested?

- I have been here for exactly one week. I was caught red-handed for selling secret documents to the foreigners. I'm now waiting to be tried.

- What is your former position?

- I used to be a lieutenant serving in the Public Security Service after several years of training. I want to get married, but I can't afford to because I'm too poor. I was caught while trying to do something to earn my living. Now I lost everything. I can't even turn to Uncle Ho or his party for help. I'm very sad. My future is so uncertain!

Thinking he was honest, I tried to console him:

- Don't worry! As young as you are, you still have a lot to learn from experience. I hope the revolutionary government will handle your case with leniency.

As a newcomer, he was in need of everything. Feeling sorry for him, I gave him a pair of shorts and some food. I then told him I would let him know why I was happy although in prison when I had a chance. I had affection for him right at the beginning when we first met. We came to understand each other better. On Sundays, I often went over to talk with him in secret, sharing his sorrows, supporting him mentally and encouraging him to keep faith in himself, especially in God and to move forward to a brighter future. I also asked him about the Communist Party, the government, and about his training period at the Public Security College, and many more. Finally, I asked:

- Did you study the book entitled "Gia Tô Bí Lục" (Secret Documents about Catholicism) during your training period?

- Yes, I did.

- What do you think about it?

- I studied the book because I had to. But I don't quite agree with what have been written in it. There are a lot of contradictions and concoctions. When in contact with the priests, I come to know they are all intellectuals and honest people, men of strong personality. You cannot hide the truth, you know.

I tried to help him in many ways, both materially and spiritually. Therefore, he became a close friend of mine, showing much affection for me. When he was released from solitary confinement to go "down there", I introduced him to a priest from Bui Chu (also his hometown) and asked my friend to help him.

In 1987, all the prisoners in the camp were allowed to gather for the celebration of Tet and to wish one another a happy New Year. During that happy occasion, he came to me with the intention of converting to Catholicism. I told my fellow priest to teach him catechism. My plan was to wait for him to be released from prison before I could baptize him. I needed some time to test his faith. He happily followed my advice.

Early in 1988, I was set free. But the former public service agent and my fellow priest were not released until the end of the year. He was released thanks to the effective intervention of his parents and influential people from his family. He was not restored however to his former position but lived a normal life as a simple citizen.

Remembering me, he left the North for the South to visit me while I was living in 3rd District, Saigon. Just released, still very poor, I tried to seek ways to satisfy him during his stay in Saigon. The only means of transportation I had at that time was a used home-made bicycle. I did not hesitate to lend it to him. My folks considered me as a "pretentious gentleman", blaming me for being too credulous. They believed that the Northerners were very poor and notorious for avidity, that they might take Honda, bicycle or anything they had borrowed from the Southerners. I answered: "Don't worry about it! If they return what they have borrowed, that's fine; if not, they can keep for themselves; no problem."

When in prison, I thought, I used to share what

I had.   Now if it happens that I lose something, I don't have to worry about it. We lose everything when we die. But as long as we live, we can create wealth again. The truth is as simple as that.

I have been in the United States for almost ten years and have never heard about him ever since. I don't know if he is baptized or not, but I am pretty sure he cannot forget the happy memories we had together in prison, especially the commitment he has made with God to become His faithful child.

X. THE DAY OF RETURN IN TRIUMPH

Three months before we moved back to camp Nam Ha, an unexpected event had happened. One of our fellow priests was allowed to move "down there", ready to go home. That lucky guy was Rev. T.V.T. We were all happy for him and none of us was surprised at the news, as he was well-known for being close to cadres who often excused him from labor. After a few weeks, he affirmatively spread the news (I really don't know what source it comes from) that other priests would be set free too, except me among the few who would never be released. At first, I felt rather sad. But thinking again, I would not mind. I have accepted to die in prison, I thought, my life remains in God's hands. Whatever happens is His will. He is my strength and my joy throughout the arduous journey of my life on earth.

Knowing father T.V.T would certainly return to Saigon, we secretly sent a letter to Archbishop Nguyen Van Binh, warning him of Rev. T.V.T's return so that he might be on guard against him.

The news spread by Rev. T.V.T that I would never be released turned out to be false. Early in 1988, all of us, including me were set free. Upon arrival at Saigon, we took turns to visit the Archbishop. He invited all of us to a reunion dinner organized in our honor right at his residence. The absence of Rev. T.V.T that day indicated that the Archbishop had been well informed of his personality. I sometimes met Rev. T.V.T afterwards. But our relationship was becoming reserved. We were no longer familiar with each other. What a shame!

Rev. T.V.T had been home for a few years before he suffered from high blood pressure and died. Archbishop Nguyen Van Binh conducted his funeral service, with the participation of quite a few priests, brothers and sisters from various congregations and organizations, particularly members of "Legio Mariae" and parishioners. Rev. T.V.T had got involved with much zeal in religious activities of the laity, and in social communications. He was especially known for the devotion of the Virgin Mary. He also used to serve as a chaplain for "Senatus Legio Mariae of Vietnam." May God and Mary have pity on him and forgive him for all his weaknesses and blunders so that he can enjoy God's holy presence forever.

After the departure of one of our friends, life in solitary confinement went on as usual. But we had a vague feeling something unusual might be happening soon. Cadres often came to us for whatever we owned. We were willing to give out almost everything in our possession, thus winning a lot of respect from them.

Exactly as expected, we were ordered to move. Where to go? We asked ourselves but nobody knew. When asked, cadres just gave an ambiguous answer. Yet, we felt more and more optimistic, because besides us, other political prisoners from the South "down there" got the order to move, too.

As I remember, the order was given out on a Thursday afternoon, when we were back from hard labor. We packed just what we really needed for the journey, leaving extra things, foods and what we could not take along, partly to secretly-ordained priests from the North, partly to cadres who had asked before, and partly to the criminal prisoners who needed most. I did not forget to tell my fellow priests to take altar-bread and wine along, leaving some to Northern priests who were still remaining. I also handed the Eucharist to some of Catholic prisoners to keep for themselves and distribute to others.

We were ready to set off, entrusting everything to Divine Providence.

As usual, three of us (Tr, Q, Th) tried to stick together in the same car. The communists always choose nighttime for us to travel. On a Friday evening, we, in group of twenty, were ordered to board the Molotovas parking in front of the main entrance. The unusual thing is that we were not bound by the shackles. Yet, many armed guards were still around. At a whistle-blowing, the convoy began to roll into the dark for an unknown destination. We told one another to say prayers and the Rosary for a safe traveling.

It was Saturday morning when we reached camp Nam Ha where we had been five years before. The distance from Thanh Cam to Nam Ha is only 200 km. Yet, rattling aged Molotovas had tortured us the whole night before arriving at Nam Ha. We were thankful to God for a safe journey. It was still early in the morning. We had to wait in line at the camp gate for the inspection of belongings before being allowed to enter the camp.

Cadres came at seven o'clock. They checked us very fast, just for form's sake. After that, we were allowed into the camp. Passing the gate, we saw a bustling crowd in the campground. It was political prisoners who just came in a great number from other camps. They were talking, calling one another and laughing noisily. At our sight, they gathered around to greet us. The meeting was so joyful. We just arrived at a designated area when Rev. Phan Phat Huon came to see me. He is my fellow Redemptorist. We used to serve as chaplains at the Special Military Zone of the Capital. I had not met him since 1975 when we left for reeducation. Years and years of suffering in prison had made us age rapidly. Yet, we felt so happy to meet again after having undergone so many trials of life. We considered it a real blessing from God to meet again alive. As Rev. Huon had come a week before, he promised to bring us some of his necessities. Thank you, Rev. Huon, for your kindness!

After a moment, people who had worked with me for "Tin Mung" movement in Camp Nam Ha, came to see me. They brought with them those who had been baptized during my absence, and presented them to me, saying: "Father, these are the products of our religious activities in camp." My heart full of joy, I congratulated them on their effort and shook hands with each of them. We marked the happy event with a Thanksgiving Sunday Mass and a friendly food party. There were altogether five converts, not to mention those coming from other priests' groups.

Ten days in camp Nam Ha had passed. Yet, we did not have to go for labor. We were free all day contacting one another. I took the opportunity to go around and talk with friends from other buildings.During our conversation, I came to understand them better and tried to help them make peace with God, clear their conscience and resolve thorny problems that lay ahead. In particular, they had to get prepared for various family problems they would face when released. From what I knew through feeding visits and from letters of their families read to me, the problems concerning their families were very complicated. So much change had taken place while they were being far from home for too long a period of time. They used to be high-ranking officers,influential,powerful, commanding and well-known persons, making a lot of money. Now, they thought, nothing is left, except the title of a former prisoner, destitute, powerless, depending, and un-known, living like a parasite, at the expense of their wives and children.Without an iron-will, especially without a strong faith to live by, how can they sur-vive such a terrible situation. They must, therefore, prepare their mind to face reality when they go home and live with their family members, hopefully to avoid a mental shock and an inferior complex about them-selves.

I have talked with a high-ranking officer. He is also a Protestant who sympathizes with Catholicism.During our conversation, I knew that when he returned home, he and his family mem-bers intended to become Catholics. (Before 1975, his wife was a lawyer). As a delicate and honest person, he said to me: "Father, the simple truth is this: "Marriage life is a succession of ups and downs. As husband and wife, we must live with them to enjoy a happy marriage. I always believe in my wife's faithfulness, rain or shine. During the long years I was in prison, she has showed patience and love for me. Father, the first thing I'll do when going home is to say to her: "Honey, you have proved to be my truthful wife by wonderfully achieving the duty of feeding me and children to keep our family in good shape. Now, thank God, I'm home. But, you know I can't do anything yet. So, please keep doing whatever you can for the family. I promise to cooperate with you and follow your order. I find it easy to do that."

He stopped talking and laughed heartily, which moved me to tears. He then added: "Don't you see, dad, that by saying so, I can level all the hurdles caused by time and space. And I am sure she will recognize in me an honest husband and a true father of our children."

When I was back to Saigon, he and his wife came to see me once. I regret not being able to find their whereabouts since I came to the United States. I always remember them in my prayers.

Actually, many practiced what they had prepared for their post-prison lives. One day, I happened to see a former high-ranking officer carrying his wife on a bicycle during their business trip in front of St. Paul hospital (now is known as Dien Bien Phu). He stopped his bicycle and said happily: "Dad, now I volunteer to be my wife's driver. Both of us, we work as itinerant vendors for a living. I can go anywhere she wants me to. We're just trying to make ends meet. We're very happy, anyway." I reacted accordingly: "That's wonderful! May God help you settle down for a new life, soon." I noticed a clear expression of joy and satisfaction on his wife's face.

Regrettably, his reunion with family did not last long before his wife fell seriously ill and died. During his absence, she had taken good care of her family, all by herself during the most tragic moment of her life, until he came home and found his family in good shape under her control. It is the will of God that after being exhausted from a wife's duties, she deserves resting in peace with Him in Heaven, leaving her family to her husband.

I came to see her when she was seriously ill. I also attended her funeral service and concelebrated a Requiem Mass for her soul. She had set a good example of a mother who spent the entire life serving her family in an unselfish way. I always admire her for such a great sacrifice. May God have pity on her!

The husband (L.D.K) and children have left for the U.S. and are now living in San Jose. I have visited them and found that their lives had been well established. Thank God!

Decree of Release Proclaimed

Since the day we entered camp Nam Ha, the rumor that political prisoners from the South would be released, was bearing more and more evidence of truth, due to the fact that cadres conspicuously changed their attitude, trying to sympathize with us and ask for what we possessed, that many delegations from the central government were sent to camp, seemingly to get prepared for something important.

As for us, we were becoming more and more optimistic and got excited about all kinds of news.

What we expected, was bound to come

At 10 o'clock in the morning, we were ordered to gather in the campground. A central delegation accompanied by the head of the camp, a lieutenant colonel, came to see us. After a few words of greeting, the head of the delegation read the decree of release and began to call one by one the name of the released. The list was long, up to thousands of people. Hearing their names, some of them jumped up ant shouted with joy. After that, the camp head told us to get packing, ready for the discharge ceremony.

By observation, I found that after the reading of the list of names, the joyful excitement of a noisy crowd subsided slowly in silence. The happy mood of many gave way to worries and anxieties before an uncertain future when they return home and live with their family members in a new environment.

They said to me: "It's okay to go home, but we don't know what the future holds for us." I answered them: "Don't worry! We can make it as long as we live. Let's have a will and a strong faith. We have survived the Communist prison. We will do better at home. With God's help, our future will be guaranteed. Let's hold on to hope and live!"

We knew that the number of those remaining in camp was more than one hundred. So we left them

273

some of our possessions, especially medicine, and to the Catholics some consecrated bread and wine for future use.

The discharge ceremony was well prepared and organized with a lot of fanfare. There were news reporters from capitalist countries such as the United States, France, Italy, Holland, Belgium, etc. not to mention those from the Communist block.

Before the opening of the ceremony, media co-respondents and news reporters interviewed many of us. A correspondent from Holland came to interview me in English:

- What's your name?
- My name is Dinh Ngoc Que.
- What are you?
- I am a priest.

My answer surprised him.

- You, a priest? Why did they capture a priest? He asked.

I tried to explain some more:

- I am a priest and also an army chaplain.

The Dutch reporter still found it difficult to understand.

- Can an army chaplain be arrested, too? He asked

How long have you been here?
- Thirteen years.
- How did they treat you during those years?
- They treated me no better than other prisoners, sometimes even worse. They hate the priests,

you know.
- What did you do during the years in prison?
- I was subjected to hard labor like anybody else.
- What is your plan after the release?
- I'm still a priest, as ever.
- Do you want to go abroad?
- I don't know yet.

He then thanked me before leaving and went to others. The Dutch reporter was really handsome and young, too young to comprehend how brutal and inhuman the Communists are. No wonder he was surprised at what he had heard.

The discharge ceremony started in the meeting hall. Guests of honor were the camp head, officials from the Ministry of the Interior, wardens from various groups in the camp, and a great number of armed soldiers. Present were quite a few guests and national as well as foreign reporters. A cadre from the organizing committee announced the opening of the ceremony. Everybody stood up to sing the National Anthem and a song entitled *"Như có Bác Hồ trong ngày vui đại thắng"* (It is likely that Uncle Ho is present on the great day of triumph.) After that the camp head began to read the decree of discharge before giving a short speech in which he extended his congratulations to us. He said that after having made progress in reeducation, we had been released to go home, thanks to the leniency of the Party and the government. He advised us to co-operate with the revolutionary government for the building of socialism, peace and prosperity of the country.

Following the head of the camp's speech, some cadres added a few more words. Finally, a chosen representative of the released stood up to say a few words of thanks to the Party, the government and the management of the camp. During the ceremony, while reporters were busy with cameras and all kinds of electronic equipments, one of them remained seated, carefully counting the number of the released, one by one to check if they were on the list and make sure truth must be kept. I had the feeling that my attendance was just for formality. My presence was there, physically, but my mind was somewhere else. Everybody was deep in thoughts. The following day, we went to the staff to receive back our possessions they had kept for us since the day we reported for reeducation such as wristwatches, gold chains and other valuable items. My automatic watch had stopped ticking apparently for missing its owner. How could I bring it back to life. So, I had to throw it away to buy a new one. The majority of us got back fake items, because the original ones had been replaced. Luckily, my gold chain remained the same. It might be that it is of little gold. Where do we go for complaint, I thought, we are released, anyway.

While we were receiving possessions back, an Italian reporter came to interview me in French. As a Catholic, he was very happy to know I was a priest. A cadre came to interrupt the interview and sent him away. Very angry, he burst out a curse "*bêtise*" and left.

During those days, I went visiting and consoling those who remained. According to what the cadres had said, the North had no place for political prisoners from the South. Therefore, the rest would be transferred to the South for a gradual release. What they had said was true. After we left, those unlucky friends were transferred to camp Ham Tan, and all of them were finally set free one by one at the end of 1992. The last ones to go were four Catholic generals (Th, Gi, T, D). Of those who were released, some wanted to stay in the North for a period of time to visit families and friends and at the same time to celebrate the Tet festival with them. Rev. DCT and I took the opportunity to visit our native village. The staff complied with our request and stamped their approval with signature at the back of the decree of release for convenience.

All the released (then free of chains) got into molotovas with open roofs and headed to Nam Dinh. They stopped at a train station where they would take the train for Saigon. The station was bustling with activities. Some got well-dressed while others were still in camp uniforms. All of us shared the same mood: happy to be free, yet, anxious about an uncertain future that is lying ahead.

As for Rev. D.C.T and I, we crossed the Tam De Bridge and took a bus for the diocese of Bui Chu. A special sightseeing tour began.

"... wherein (we) shall greatly rejoice, if now

(we) must be for a little time made sorrowful in diverse temptations:

That the trial of (our) faith (much more precious than gold which is tried by the fire) may be found into praise and glory and honor at the appearing of Jesus Christ, whom having not seen (we) love: in whom also now (we) see him not, (we) believe: and believing shall rejoice with joy unspeakable and glorified; Receiving the end of (our) faith, even the salvation of (our) souls."

(St. Peter, I, 6 – 9)

When I went to report for reeducation, my colleague Nguyen Ngoc Lan warned me: "You're going to carry ties and rails", implying that I would be subjected to hard labor. I pointed to his face, replying: "My friend, I accept to die in prison. If not, I will return in triumph."

In 1988, when I returned, everything had changed. My friend had unfrocked himself, denouncing his priesthood, got married and had a daughter. As for me, thank the Lord, I continue to follow God who has called me to serve Him and the human souls. I was happy to carry "ties and rails" with others and share with them joys and sorrows. I have been released and are now living in the United States. Although far from home, I feel joyful because I have surrendered myself to God and served my fellow men to the best of my abilities.

January 18th, 1998

XI. A SPECIAL SIGHTSEEING TOUR

Since I left my native village for the Imperial City of Hue to start my high school in 1946 (42 years ago), I had never had a chance to return. According to Communist propaganda, the socialist North is very civilized in every aspect. I wanted to see it with my own eyes. I knew my family, relatives and friends were looking forward to seeing me when they heard of the news of my release. So, I was determined to stay in the North for one month to satisfy my curiosity. When everybody arrived at the train station in Nam Dinh, those who did not want to stay, were given a ticket for Saigon.

On the way to the seat of Bui Chu Diocese

Rev. D.C.T and I, we took a bus for Bui Chu to visit the Bishop of the diocese. The road was not long but scarred with potholes. So, we did not reach the destination until it was very late in the evening. We got down the bus and groped our way to the Bishop's residence. It was dark and the church area was deserted. We pulled the bell several times but nobody answered the gate. We turned back and went over to the convent of nuns. We pulled the gate bell again and again. Nobody was in sight. It was too late for the nuns to go out. We were thinking of staying overnight at some nearby inn when we saw a man riding a bicycle on the way to the bishop's residence. He got off the bicycle and asked us: "Where are you both going in the dark like this?" We replied: "We're looking for a place to stay over-night. Can you help?" He said: "I think, you can find some place around here in the village." He then turned his back, leaving us alone in the dark. No sooner had we walked a short distance than we heard a call from behind. It was the bicycle man. He returned and said:

- I just wonder if any of you is a priest.

- I am, and so is my friend. I answered.

- Pardon me, fathers, I can't recognize you. I am a priest, too.

- We don't know you are a priest, either.

- Aren't you afraid of the dark?

- We're former political prisoners from the South, just released, you know. We would like to come here to visit the bishop before going back to our native village for the celebration of Tet. We've just pulled the bell of the bishop's residence, but nobody answered. We also went to the convent, but no nuns appeared. We were planning to find a place to stay overnight, waiting for tomorrow to see the bishop, when we met you.

- You're very lucky to meet me. If you stay over-night at a villager's house, you must report at local authorities first, which is very inconvenient. Now, I invite you to follow me to the bishop's residence.

After saying "Thanks", I stepped back and let Rev. D.C.T converse with him. I just wondered why I was not able to identify him as a priest. At a closer look, I found that he did wear a cassock. But to ease his bicycle-riding he had lifted the garment up to the waist and opened up his collar. Therefore I could not identify him as a priest, especially, when we were in the dark.

Once in his room, I realized he was a manager for the diocese. He was still young, about 40. He switched on the lights before leading us into the reception room well furnished with meticulously carved pieces of furniture, a cupboard and a refrigerator. At the corner of the room was a brand-new Dream Honda. He made tea for us. He also opened the refrigerator to treat us to lean pork paste and a square glutinous rice cake (bánh chưng) (Tet was drawing near). What a polite and caring person! He made us feel at home and saw to it that we had comfortable places to sleep. Left alone, we felt free to use the food he had provided. Due to hunger, we ate with much appetite, especially after an exhausting journey. After bed arrangement was done, he came back with three other priests to converse with us. We talked about many things. Knowing we were Southern priests just released from prison, they openly revealed to us what should be kept secret from the outsiders. I came to know many sad stories about bishop Cung, Bishop Tinh, about the difficult situation of the clergy and the laity as well. Briefly speaking, Northern people were starving slowly, as the result of a deteriorating economy. The manager also let me know that two acres of land which had been used as a garden and playing ground for the seminarists, were then turned into a rice-field for the seat of the diocese.

We talked and talked without caring to sleep. During our conversation, a young man came and said to the manager: "Father, the bishop is now in Trung Linh. He wants two visiting priests to stay here, waiting for him. He'll be back tomorrow morning to meet them." I was rather surprised at his report. But the manager calmed me down: "I have sent for the bishop. If he says so, both of you just stay here with us, tonight."

Not surprisingly, living with the Communists, one has to be careful and discreet. We did not go to bed until after midnight.

The next morning, we had to get up at four. In the North, parishioners usually go to church very early for the morning Mass before they begin their shopping and farming activities. We celebrated Mass the first time after being released in the sacristy of the cathedral of Bui Chu diocese, our native place.

During the Holy Mass, I felt overwhelmed with joy and happiness as my heart was deeply touched by God's love. Jesus had been carrying me and my friends day and night through 13 years in Communist prisons. Our Heavenly Father had protected and liberated us from all kinds of evils and finally led us to safety. To me, Divine Providence is not just a mere feeling, but something very intimate, very concrete, something tangible.

The Holy Spirit is my strength. During the difficult years in prison, I succeeded in spreading the words of God to my friends, and particularly in bringing the Eucharist to them. I did act, but it was not me who acted. Rather, it was the Holy Spirit who acted within me.

Therefore, during the Mass, I became emotional many times. Really, the first Mass I celebrated outside prison that day was an experience I can never forget.

After the Mass, we returned to the bishop's residence to have breakfast. As it rained rather heavily, I proposed that the bishop should not come back but stay in Trung Linh, waiting for us to go to see him and visit the place for convenience. The manager agreed.

We then went to the convent to visit the nuns. They welcomed us with open arms. The convent was rather large for a small number of nuns, mostly old. Novices lived in hiding. During the day, they came for training, and went home for the night. For those whose home was far away, they were allowed to stay overnight, but they must always be on the alert, like animals who were being hunted. As they said, they readily sacrificed themselves for the Kingdom of Heaven. There was nothing to be afraid of.

How brave they are!

To Trung Linh

We left the priests and the nuns for Trung Linh to visit the bishop. The manager lent each of us a bicycle as a means of transportation and had a person accompany us as a guide. We got on bicycle and rode off down a slippery road under the cold rain. I lost my balance and almost fell off several times. I had not ridden a bicycle for a long time, you know. I felt sorry for Rev. D.C.T when I saw him ride with so much difficulty. We made it safely to the destination, finally.

Followed by a number of priests and nuns, the bishop went out to welcome us heartily. We talked and laughed easily. Upon entering a room, we saw a tray of delicacies prepared with Northern cuisine, ready for us. The bishop had lunch already. He said to us: "You must be hungry now. Help yourselves, please! Food is hard to come by in prison." He stood beside us, continually urging us to take more and more food. He was showing so much affection for us.

As an 80-year-old, he was really a father figure. He was known as a bishop of limited formal education (a former cathecist.) Still, everybody loved him for his paternal qualities and virtues.

After lunch, with the bishop as a guide, we made a tour around Trung Linh area. We visited the parish, the church, the convent, especially my former boarding school which was then war-devastated. When I looked at the school sight lying in ruins among poor hamlets, my childhood memories rushed back to my mind as vivid as ever, which made my heart sink. Since the day the Communists arrived, my country had nothing to gain, but everything to lose. During the conversation, the bishop revealed to us the real situation of his diocese. The number of the faithful was too large for a restricted number of priests. In some areas, a priest must be in charge of seven or eight parishes. As a result, he was able to go only few times a year to each parish for the Mass. Pastoral demand exceeded the supply.Yet, there was no solution to that. The Communist government did not allow the needed recruitment of seminarists. They did not allow enough of them to be ordained to the priesthood either. In other words, the permit was just given out in drops. As bamboo trees grow old, shoots come up. But in reality, bamboo trees keep growing old while shoots do not come up. Though the diocese was in such a difficult situation, it still survived thanks to God's protection and His divine providence.

To Quan Cong

We talked with the bishop till evening when Rev. N. came. He had been in prison with me before. Hearing the news, he came and asked the bishop for the permission to take us to Quan Cong, his native village. We said goodbye to the bishop and the sisters and thanked them for a warm welcome before leaving for Quan Cong. Father N. carried me on his Honda while father D.C.T took the back seat of another Honda driven by a young man. We traveled across an expanse of rice fields, feeling refreshed in the country air. It was almost dark when we arrived. A bedroom was ready for us. After dinner, we talked and talked until very late in the night before going to bed. All that he said really satisfied my curiosity. Father N. and I promised to meet in Saigon, some day.

The following morning, we celebrated Mass at father N's residence. As a rule, priests released from prison were not allowed to perform pastoral duties in public. During the Mass, we prayed for each other to have enough patience and courage to serve God and our brothers and sisters.

To Phu Nhai

After breakfast, father N. requested two young men to take us to Phu Nhai by Honda. Phu Nhai temple is a colossal structure, the largest church in Indochina, I might say. The church, built in Gothic style, was dedicated to the Virgin Mary of Immaculate Conception to honor the bishops' promise with St. Mary after they had been saved from a fierce persecution. The building is so beautiful. Still, so many years have passed without it being upgraded or improved.

We went to the parish to see the pastor (Rev. Th) Father Th. greeted us very warmly. After a moment of friendly talk, father D.C.T left us to visit his relatives living right in the village of Phu Nhai where he was born. Before going, Rev. D.C.T promised to meet me in Nam Dinh, soon.

Left alone, I felt free to talk with the pastor. He was of a big, strong build. He was serving as a director of vocations for the diocese. If he had had more chance to learn, he would have achieved much more. He was so smart and prestigious. He showed me around the parish. Everything was well-organized and in proper order. Knowing for sure he was open-minded, and quick to learn, I brought up various subjects on how to train future seminarists (I talked from experience with secretly-ordained priests while in prison,) how to raise the standard of education for the young Catholics (I talked from experience as of a high school principal and director while in Saigon before 1975). We agreed totally on how a new society should be. To improve the economy is relatively easy whereas to restore a depraved society to a better one is much more difficult. With a strong determination, a solid unity and a long-term commitment, we can make all the difference.

The next morning, I had the honor of celebrating Mass in the sisters' chapel. In prison when celebrating Mass in secret, I used to dress very casually, in shorts, with a T-shirt, whatever, just to hide what I was doing. A clean-washed bottle of "Tiger balm" could replace the chalice. A crumb of bread, a drop of wine would do. That day, however, I was dressed in white. The well-lit altar was draped with carefully ironed, spotless white sheets. The gilded chalice and plates were shining under the candlelight. In such an environment, I was suddenly moved to tears. I could not help it, because I experienced such a boundless love my Heavenly Father had for me. That God comes down on this altar graced with all kinds of ornaments is a normal thing, but that he comes down to me in prison, on a humble place deprived of decorations is what I am not able to comprehend. Only when I love him in return, can I understand somewhat the mysterious love he has for me.

I asked the sisters to excuse me for the sudden outbreak of emotion before starting the Holy Mass. After the Gospel reading, I shared with the sisters my feeling on God's fatherly love. As a father, he had comforted, protected and carried me to safety through the last 13 years of prison till now. Finally I thanked the sisters for their prayers when I was in prison.

When the Mass ended, the sisters sang: "Mother, please console us always..." Again, I wept, touched by the motherly love Mary had reserved for me.

When having breakfast with the sisters, I recounted a few stories in prison, making them laugh heartily.

To Quan Phuong

I went back to father Th. After lunch, he had a young man carry me on Honda to Quan Phuong and Ninh Cuong. Knowing I was a Southern priest just released from prison, two other young men also wanted to join our company by Honda. The caravan therefore was four persons and two Hondas. As young men, full of vigor, they traveled at full speed. Sometimes I had to slow them down for safety. We stopped by the seminary of Quan Phuong where so many seminarists of older generations had been trained to be priests. Situated on a large area of land, the imposing building looked empty and deserted. Not daring to get in, we just made a tour around for observation, and then continued our trip to Ninh Cuong.

To Ninh Cuong

At nightfall, we reached the parish of Ninh Cuong where I met a lanky person, about 30 years of age. I asked him for the pastor. As I dressed casually, with near-sighted glasses and a felt-hat with flaps over my ears, he looked at me from head to toe with a perplexed expression on his face, saying with determination: "The pastor is not in, sir. Please, go somewhere else." The young man who carried me on Honda, intervened: "This is a priest." I then seized the opportunity to reassure him:"I am a Redemptorist, just released from prison. On the way back to Lieu De, my native village to celebrate Tet, I would like to stop by to visit the pastor here." Recovered from perplexity, he lowered his voice, saying: "Let me go find the pastor for you, father." Just a few minutes later, the pastor appeared. He invited me into a reception room and talked with me in a very friendly manner. I walked out to thank the young men for a safe ride. They shook hands with me and returned to Phu Nhai during the night. They assured me that they had been used to driving in the dark. I wished them "bon voyage" and then walked back to talk with the pastor. He was the classmate of the diocese's manager and the pastor of Phu Nhai. They were among those who had been ordained in secret by bishop Tinh. They were permitted to perform pastoral duties in public, except one still in the seat of the diocese of Bui Chu.

The pastor invited me to stay overnight and then had the church bell rung, announcing the Mass to be celebrated the next morning by a visiting priest.

The Mass started at 4:00 in the morning. The news of a visiting priest drew quite a big crowd, amounting to about 4,500 people. The church was well organized under the direction of the pastor. The Mass was highlighted by a well-trained group of children dancing and offering gifts, and music accompanied with various instruments. I had the feeling I was celebrating 3 p.m. mass for children at the parish of the Mother of Perpetual Help in Saigon. That day, I heard confessions before celebrating Mass. I shared God's words with the pastor as a concelebrant. It was the first time after being released from prison, I celebrated Mass in a church in public. Therefore, my father's friends and my mother's relatives recognized me. After Mass, they came to see me and invite me to their homes for an early celebration of Tet. I could only go to Mrs. Trum Rinh's house, my mother's younger sister to celebrate the new Year with her family. They greeted me with a long string of firecrackers.

As it was a day before the New Year's eve, I had to ask the pastor for permission to leave for Lieu De in order to celebrate Tet in time.

To Quan Lieu

The pastor of Ninh Cuong parish allowed three young men to accompany me to Lieu De. I said good bye to the pastor and thanked him for a warm reception he had reserved for me before starting off. Two Hondas were travelling parallel with each other. We had to take a ferry-boat across the Ninh Co River to Lieu De. The young men let me know that Lieu De parish had no pastor as there was no replacement for the pastor who had died long time ago. Therefore Rev. D., the pastor of Quan Lieu parish must be concurrently in charge. Once a week, he had to go over to Lieu De for the Sunday Mass. I then asked the young men to take me to Quan Lieu to report to Rev. D. They happily complied with my request. Arriving at Quan Lieu, I went to see the pastor and asked him for permission to celebrate Mass and perform the holy sacraments at Lieu De, my native village during the time I stayed there. He happily agreed and promised to go to Lieu De to see me. After that, I left him for my native village.

To Lieu De for Tet celebration

My birthplace is a large village of about 5000 residents. There are a communal house and a nearby market place for the whole area. My village is now a townlet, district of Truc Ninh. After the 1954 exodus, the Communists confiscated my relatives' houses and used them as local government offices.

This is the place where I was born and my mother died (in 1942). In the old days, my parents' residence comprised a 5-partition main building and 9-partition supplementary quarters. Now the main building remains the same. The only difference is that the thatch-roof has been replaced by red tiles. As for the supplementary quarters, there are only a 2-partition kitchen and a pigsty left. The front brick yard and a garden are still there. A large fishpond at the back remains unchanged. All the fruit trees around the house are nowhere to be seen. In 1954, my father and family fled to the South, leaving to my aunt named Dinh Thi Phuc all his assets. When I came home, she was almost eighty, living with the family of her younger brother in the house my father had left. Though I did not let her know my home-coming in advance, she was still able to recognize me. As for my younger brothers' and sisters children, none of them could recognize me. My father's neighbors only heard that he had a son who had been ordained to the priesthood. Everybody was so happy to see me in person, especially on the Lunar New Year's eve. I told my relatives to ask permission from the local authority for me to celebrate the Mass at church as the pastor had given me the right to take his place. My younger brothers took me to the local authority, but nobody wanted to be held responsible for the decision. I let them know I was Mrs Phuc's nephew and carried a permit from the Ministry of the Interior, allowing me to return to my native village.

After reading the permit and discussing with one another, they came to a conclusion, saying: "As you have the permit to stay at Mrs. Phuc's house, you can do there whatever you want." We said a few words of thanks and left. Back home, I said to my brothers: "I will celebrate Mass right here, at our house every day during the first three New Year's days. Please, let everybody know that I would like to invite them all."

At the news of my presence, the elders in the village came to greet me. Knowing that I was not allowed to celebrate the Mass in the church, the parishioners got rather upset at first. But thinking again, they were happy to have Mass anyway.

A great number of people gathered at my aunt's house for Mass preparations. They surrounded the house with strings of banners. They even hung red scrolls of Tet parallel sentences to greet me. During the Mass, the altar was lit up with candles and decorated with gorgeous flowers. The Holy Mass was also highlighted by a rather well-trained choir.

On the New Year's eve, the air was filled with the sounds of firecrackers. My relatives spent the whole night, talking. They only went home at daybreak to get ready for the 10 a.m. Mass on the first New Year's Day.

That morning, parishioners crowded to our home. The house, the yard, the entranceway were jammed with people. They even spilled into the garden, trampled on vegetables, vying for room before the Mass started. We respected their devotion and let them feel at home, even at the small expense of our family economy.

The crowd swelled beyond our expectation. During the New Year Mass, on behalf of all people present, I offered Thanks to God for the past year and prayed for a peaceful and happy New year. I also prayed for my ancestors, my relatives, particularly for my own mother. The Mass was punctuated by incense-burning ceremony, gift-offering ritual and a choir singing heart-touching hymns I had not heard for a long time. After the Mass, quite a few stayed with me for a friendly talk and did not leave till noon.

After having lunch with my family members, I followed my aunt to visit my younger brothers, and some of my relatives and wish them a happy New Year.

On the second and third New Year day, the Mass crowd was about as large as the first one. Every day, after meal, my aunt took me to places where I had spent my childhood with a lot of cherished memories, places where my mother's parents used to live, especially to St. Dinh Viet Du's tomb, a fore-father in my family line. According to my aunt's words, the saint's temple had been hit by American bombs. Nothing was left but his statue and a wall behind it. The parishioners had brought the statue to the church and installed it on the altar. I still kept my photo taken by the side of his statue for souvenir.

Actually, I returned to my native village that time for two purposes:

First, to visit the tomb of Saint martyr Dinh Viet Du, our family's forefather to express my heart-felt thanks to him. His courage and strong faith had helped me go through all those years in prison, and also to show my filial piety toward my own mother. Before she died, she had held my hand, saying: "Everyday, I go to Saint Dinh Viet Du's tomb to pray for you to persevere in following your vocation." It is thanks to my mother's prayers and to Saint Dinh Viet Du's advocation that I have been chosen to be among God's ministers.

I always follow my mother's example in honoring

the Vietnamese martyrs, thus receiving from them abundant blessings.

Second, to visit my own mother's tomb who died in 1942. Thanks to her persistent plea, my father had allowed me to enter religious life. I was his only son at that time and as you know, according to Vietnamese tradition, the son's duty in the family is to maintain the family line, especially in a family as great as mine. Therefore it was hard for my father to allow me such a favor. My second purpose however was not achieved as planned, because the Communists had moved the remains of my mother and those of other villagers to some place nobody knew. I returned to Saigon with a deep regret. Instead, God was going to grant me an even greater blessing.

An omen during the dream from a dead person

My mother knows I am back to my native village to celebrate Tet and visit her tomb and, if possible, to exhume her body and transfer it to Saigon. But God wants otherwise.

I returned to Saigon in early 1988, and reluctantly went to the United States in early 1993. When my step mother died (11/09/1993), I was not able to go home. Luckily, my younger brother's wife named Nguyen Thi Mai who was living in The United States, represented us to go home for her funeral. The story I am going to tell is a kind of mystery to me.

While my step mother was still living, as a good and delicate person, my dead mother did not want to cause inconvenience to anybody. She waited till early 1994 when my step mother's funeral service was over before telling an omen to a public security office chief while he was sleeping. The omen indicated that my mother's tomb was still somewhere in his zone. He started the search, and at 8:00 a.m. on Oct 16th, (of the Lunar Year) found a tombstone inscribed with the following words: "Maria Phac, 42 years old, died on 2/16/44." It's undoubtedly my mother.

Thanks to my mother's beneficial influence, many public security agents won the lottery. To show gratitude, they offered stipends for a mass-intention for her soul. My aunt Phuc let my father living in Ho Nai know the story. And in no time, my father sent the information to me in the United States. I was then determined to have my two younger sisters (Dinh Thi Nu and Dinh Thi Hue) go North to find out, and if possible, to bring my mother's remains back to my father. On Dec 29, 1994, as requested, my two sisters brought my mother's remains to Ho Nai where my father was living.

Following is the original paper handwritten by Mr. Vo Duc Viet, an eyewitness of what had happened so miraculously, concerning my mother's tombstone, so that together with my family, you could offer thanks to God for having reunited our family.

A Miraculous Tombstone
Twenty-one days had passed since the public

security district office destroyed the old building to build a new one. During that period, the office faced many difficulties, and those who worked for the office suffered heavy financial loss.

On October 16 (of the Lunar Year) the chief of the office was given an omen during his dream, telling him to look for a tomb in his area. He began searching and at 8 a.m. found a tombstone which read as follows: "Maria Phuc, 42 years old, died on 2/16/44." The tombstone was broken, with a crucifix sculptured in relief and the number 1955 at the back. After the tombstone was washed clean and pieced together with cement, a number of public security agents brought fresh flowers and incense, asking for forgiveness and praying for success and prosperity in business. That very night, all of them hit the last two numbers of the first prize they had bet on (Số Đề number 16.) Before such a miraculous happening, those who were serving in the office came to Mr. And Ms. Viet, asking to offer their contributions for a mass-intention for her soul. After that, all of them, and also those who had heard about or seen the tombstone, hit "Số Đề" for several days in a row. The last two numbers of the first prize they bet on, coincided with the numbers inscribed on the tombstone. Four days later, her family asked permission to move her remains, a captain came with incense and bowed to the tombstone, asking for her protection before she went (on Sunday). Miraculously, he hit the 14 million jackpot on Saturday evening.

After Mrs. Phac's tombstone with her remains was discovered, the office ground was always swarmed with those people who had benefited from her answer to their prayers, and the air around was embalmed with the fragrance of burning incense.

Thirteen days later, (Nov. 20, 1994), the captain was told in his dream that the tombstone was not laid in the right position and direction. The following morning, he hurried to the office ground to burn incense in her honor and asked her permission to readjust her tombstone in the right direction. Again, he hit the 14 million jackpot that very day. Therefore, everybody in the public security office, including high-ranking officials wished to rebuild her tomb at the office with their contributions to public funds for the convenience of honoring her.

Her body is just a few remaining bones but her soul is very responsive to people's prayers. She always stands beside her offsprings, keeping them under her safe protection.

As an extensive traveler for 36 years, I have seen many things, but I have never witnessed such a mysterious happening in my life.

Her tombstone was installed in 1955. One month later (Feb 16, 1954) when people were back to rebuild their parents' tombs and reinstalled the stones, a number of officials in the office who were in charge, hit the number 55 again on that day.

It is a miraculous event that has never happened before. I am lucky enough to know the details of the story at the very beginning when her tombstone was discovered. Now I would like to jot down these lines without going into specifics. One thing I know for sure is that her soul is very responsive to prayers. I hope when witnessing this miraculous event, we, as her offsprings might come to worship God and pray for her protection as long as we live on earth.

Lieu De, Dec. 20, 1994
Vo Duc Viet, Mr. And Ms. Duong's son
Mr. And Ms. Cai Ru's nephew

Home address: 05/KT, Lieu De Village

* I just retrace blurred letters in the original copy without altering it.
January 23rd, 1998
Dinh Ngoc Que, CSSR

My father died on March 30, 1996. The following day, my two younger brothers (Thu and Truat) and I left the United States for Vietnam to take care of his funeral. After that, we simultaneously built three tombs: one for my father, one for my mother and one for my younger brother Dinh Xuan Thi (Xuong). I also blessed these three tombs before returning to the United States.

Now I am very satisfied at the idea that I have fulfilled my filial duty, especially to my own mother, who, by means of an omen, has informed us of her tomb, and helped us realize the reunion of our family in the South.

Thanks be to God for ever and ever.

To Nam Dinh and then Bao Dap

One the third day of Tet, a farewell party was held in my honor in the afternoon. I said good bye to my aunt Phuc, my brothers and their families and all the villagers before leaving for Nam Dinh by Honda accompanied by another one.

I returned to my native village after 42 years of absence and stayed there just about three days before leaving. I had to go, by all means, to answer the call of my vocation as a priest, my heart heavy with all kinds of sentimental attachments. I recalled having the same feeling when, with my father's permission, I left home in 1946, just two years after my mother's death, to join the Congregation of the Redemptorists. And I went with determination without even turning my head back.

Indeed, without God's help, all my efforts would come to nothing.

We arrived at Nam Dinh before sundown, thanks to the Honda drivers who had the skill of weaving in and out between potholes on the road. I said thanks to the drivers and left them for Nam Dinh parish. I introduced myself to the pastor and asked him to let me stay overnight. He welcomed me very warmly.

The next morning, I celebrated Mass in private. After having breakfast with the pastor, I asked his permission to go visiting the city of Nam Dinh, especially the monastery of the Redemptorists near Lake Raket.

This is the city where I had spent my childhood with my maternal grandfather. I had also lived in the monastery a week before being admitted to the Juvenat of Hue. The city then looked old and dirty, with no additional buildings and also for lack of repairs due to war.

I had a hard time finding the monastery because the area was invaded by city-dwellers.

Actually, what remained were only a chapel and an apartment complex for some Redemptorists. Religious activities were very limited for lack of priests. I went back to the parish at noontime and, with the pastor, went to Bao Dap to celebrate the Silver Anniversary of ordination to the priesthood of the Pastor of Báo Đáp' Parish.

Bao Dap village in Bui Chu was once well-known for business of dyeing silk and fabrics. As the trade professionals had left for the South in 1954, the business was in the doldrums. The parish was rather well-organized by a relatively young pastor. The church and the rectory looked more imposing than other places. We ate meal with the pastor and returned to Nam Dinh for the night, ready to go to Hanoi, the following morning.

To Hanoi

We boarded a bus and reached Hanoi at 2:00 p.m. We went straight to Cardinal Trinh Van Can's

302

residence. The Cardinal with other priests welcomed us very warmly. We planned to stay for a week. The Cardinal's residence was inspected that night. The next morning, the Cardinal jokingly said to me: "Listen, father Que! My house has not been inspected for a long time, and now it is, after you came and stayed just the first night." Upon those words, he laughed with pleasure.

We concelebrated Mass with him at his own chapel in the morning. We had lunch with the Cardinal and other priests in his residence. While eating, he told us many stories, two of which were considered as predictions that, to my knowledge, have proved true.

The first story was about the temple of the Mother of Perpetual Help at Thai Ha Hamlet. The Cardinal said to me: "Go back to Saigon and let your superiors know that I don't want to lose the temple at Thai Ha. I recommend that old father Bich be replaced. He is too old and weak to manage the temple, and his vision is very poor, too. You know, to me the temple is really a treasure in my diocese. Or you, father Que, you can stay with us, can't you?"

I replied: "Your Excellency, I am always ready. But, as a priest just released from prison, I doubt the government will allow me."

The Cardinal had passed away and now the temple at Thai Ha is being run by another priest from the South. The place is busy with more religious activities than before.

The reason why the Communist government allowed no other orders such as Dominican and Franciscan orders to go North but our Congregation is that in 1954, Dominican and Franciscan orders moved all their priests and friars to the South, while the Congregation of the Redemptorists still left three priests and two brothers behind. It is according to Divine Providence that our Mother of Perpetual Help must stay for ever at her sacred temple at Thai Ha with her poor, suffering children in the North.

The second story is related to the canonization of 117 Vietnamese martyrs. The cardinal said to me: "Everyone of us in the North agrees on this, whereas in the South, some, particularly the "State-owned priests, cooperate with the government, trying to stop it, or at least to exclude a number of names from the list. As for me, I am absolutely in favor of the canonization of all 117 martyrs." He then added: "Let's pray persistently for this matter. It is the glory of God, the honor of Vietnam, and particularly the encouragement of Vietnamese Catholics."

On June 19, 1988, Pope John Paul II canonized all 117 Vietnamese Martyrs. The whole catholic world rejoiced. The great event was known the world over through the media. There were no representatives of the Vietnam government. Why? The answer can be interpreted in different ways. But, in reality, it is very regrettable, because this is a pride, not only for the Catholics, but also for the whole country.

During one-week stay in Hanoi, I went back to Thai Ha hamlet to see father Bich, a colleague of mine who had volunteered to stay behind with two other priests and brothers in 1954. Ater the two Canadian priests had been banished and two other brothers were captured and died in prison, father Bich was left alone to take care of the temple.

He said to me: "Only our Mother and God can help us keep the temple and survive until now..." (1954 – 1988). Worship service is held in honor of the Mother of Perpetual Help every Saturday; and on Sundays, there is Mass for the faithful around the area and pilgrims. The whole place including the Novitiate, the Learning Institute and the rectory, was confiscated and turned into a medical center named Thai Ha Hamlet hospital. They left to father Bich only the temple, the chapel and built a small house nearby for him. The area was invaded illegally. Houses were built in disorder around, blocking the view of the parish and the temple. It was the first time I returned since 1950. Only through the guidance of a priest who carried me on his Honda, was I able to find the place.

Father Bich and I, we had a long talk. His concern was to find someone to replace him. I really admired him for his diligence and courage. I just went to the temple for a visit; I had to return to the Cardinal, for convenience.

While in Hanoi, I took the opportunity to revisit

the places of my youth: the cathedral of Hanoi, the Ham Long parish where I used to serve as an altar-boy at the time Cardinal Trinh Nhu Khue was still the pastor of the parish.

I also went to a high building near the France-Asie bank on Gia Long street where my family used to live, to Lake "Seven Acres", to Ba Dinh area, lake of the returned sword and the tramway station, to the post office, the opera house of Hanoi, Dong Xuan market and some other sights.

I even went to as far as Long Bien bridge, Gia Long new bridge, West lake, Truc Bach Lake, Dong Da mound, one-pillar pagoda...

All the places of the old times remained almost the same, except Ba Dinh area with Ho Chi Minh mausoleum and foreign embassies.

During my stay in Hanoi, I contacted quite a few city-dwellers. They seemed not to belong to Hanoi. Their unsmiling faces were lined with anxieties, their hearts devoid of hope. Most of them were dressed in * áo bà ba* (black loose shirt) and black trousers. When asked, they just said a few words in reply and hurried away.

No more was the pride of Hanoi residents of the old times. How could they rejoice while living in such a glooming environment? Hanoi had been my favorite city, but then I felt I had pity for Hanoi.

To the Imperial City of Hue
We left Hanoi for Hue to officially set foot in the

South land after thirteen years of separation. I stayed at the monastery of the Redemptorists where I had been trained as a Juveniste (1946 – 1950). The monastery area including the Juvenat, which had been very large, was then occupied by only two old priests (Father Lanh and father Diep). Both of them were in charge of the parish of the Mother of Perpetual Help. The parish church was built by our Congregation in ancient Vietnamese style. It is considered by the government as a wonder of the city for its impressive beauty, representing something typical of Vietnam.

During my 10-day stay at Hue, I tried to do whatever I could to help the two priests: celebrating Mass, preaching, presiding over retreat-sessions for various organizations, hearing the confessions, holding meetings, conducting worship services in honor of the Mother of Perpetual Help on Saturdays... I did my job passionately, unaware of the fact that I had just been released from prison.

To show affection for a priest who had just been set free, parishioners brought me a dozen of duck-eggs every evening for the improvement of my health. Hue people are poor materially but very rich sentimentally. Besides pastoral ministries, I spent my leisure-time visiting various historical places in town. The inner city where the ancient emperors had resided, remained almost the same, without any face-lift or repair. Thuong Tu gate was still there, as old as ever, with the one-yellow-star red flag streaming in the wind.

Trang Tien bridge spanning the Perfume River was rusty, due to lack of new paint. On both ends of the bridge, some remaining phoenix-tailed trees without usually red blossoms, looked so desolate. The river flowed lazily in silence as if to miss so many heroic episodes of the founding fathers in the past. Standing on Trang Tien Bridge, I let my eyes travel beyond the Perfume River to as far as Mount Ngu Binh looming bare as if in white mourning cloth. It is a natural beauty perfectly fit for the emperors.

I went visiting royal tombs such as Tu Duc's, Khai Dinh's etc... I also went to Nam Giao altar. To my remembrance, every three years, Emperor Bao Dai came here with his royal court to offer gifts to Heaven on his people's behalf and to pray for peace and prosperity of the nation. While performing that ritual, he was considered as the son of God. Nowadays, nobody cares about that meaningful tradition, and consequently Nam Giao altar had been abandoned. Even worse, it had been destroyed and replaced by a war memorial. Non-politically speaking, an ancient historical site had been regrettably lost.

Finally, I went visiting Thien An where St. Benedict's abbey was located. The abbot went out to welcome me. There were very few priests left. The abbey had been dispersed. The big loss the abbey had suffered was thousands of precious books being burned, particularly those related to the history and culture of Vietnam. The friars were trying hard to get on their feet again. And thanks to prayers and sacrifices, they survived. The abbot said: "God has let me see the light at the end of the tunnel." Being dispersed, the abbey was able to establish two more places: one at Ban Me Thuot and another at Thu Duc province. More places means more vocations. Divine providence had truly worked in a mysterious way.

Back to Saigon

It was time to be back to Saigon. We said good bye to the two priests and promised to return to help them. The promise however never materializes due to the Communist system of family census book, especially because I am an ex-prisoner. We have to stay where we are. Another power is needed for a change.

To me, that power is my God. Everything will happen, I believe, according to His providence. That's the reason why my friends (H.O) and I are now present in the United States. And, who knows, we might be back some day to serve our country.

February 2nd, 1998.

XII. TO THE UNITED STATES FOR PLEASURE

I set foot in the United States at noontime, on Jan. 12, 1993 while it was raining heavily. People said I had brought rain to California. It might be true, because since the day I came, the Californians were able to use water freely. They did not have to ration water as before, because there was abundance of rain.

Do we go to the United States to enjoy?

Yes, we go to the U.S. to enjoy, and, I think it is legitimate to do so, too.

We come here to enjoy freedom

Enjoy material things in abundance,

Enjoy what high-tech can afford,

Enjoy human rights fully...

In my opinion, however, we have to pay a price, sometimes very high, for what we want to enjoy.

We come here not only to enjoy but also to serve some other purposes.

An interview on "The Light of Faith" TV show on Jan 18, 1993.

Question 1: Does the Socialist government bring an ideal spring to our people as they wish?

Answer: The question is rather delicate. My answer is this: After being released from prison, I have celebrated Tet for four years. Each time, I have firecrackers, rice-cakes, onion-pickles, red parallel sentences, apricot-blossoms and flower markets... Whatever the tradition requires. But Spring in the true sense of the word, is still far, far away. The reason is simple. Our country is still very poor, freedom still limited in every aspect, people still face an uncertain future.

Question 2: How is the situation of the Catholics in particular?

Answer: Generally speaking, most Vietnamese Catholics keep their faith even in a difficult circumstance. Some however, give up their faith under the pressure of the new situation. Yes, I do know some people in Vietnam have abandoned their religion. But, to be honest, though I have just come to the U.S. I also notice that a number of Catholics here have lost their faith, too.

312

Question 3:   _What do the Catholics in Vietnam expect from their spiritual leaders and what do they request from the Communist government of Vietnam?_

Answer: What they expect or require is something relative. Their primary expectation is that spiritual leaders should unanimously voice a stronger demand for freedom of practicing religion, freedom of recruiting seminarists, freedom of ordaining them to the priesthood and freedom of appointing priests. They request the government to adopt a unified and open policy of treating the Catholics fair, to consider them as other citizens who have the right to live and practice their own religion. Such a fair treatment will certainly help them become a better Catholic and a better citizen, too.

Question 4:   _What is your dream when leaving Vietnam for the U.S.?_

Answer: My dream is simple. My life is always the same. I am a priest. As a priest, my primary duty is to serve God above all and to serve my brothers and sisters, particularly my compatriots living abroad to the best of my abilities. Wherever I go in the U.S., I always encourage people (including the Catholics) to turn their mind to their homeland. I use every possible means to achieve that goal.

A Thanksgiving Mass

The Nguoi Viet Daily News has announced my Thansgiving Mass as follows:

A special Thanksgiving Mass for Rev. Dinh Ngoc Que.

Westminster (NV): Thanksgiving is a festival celebrated annually in November by the Americans to mark the first days they landed on the new continent and succeeded in becoming a great nation.

This year, a special Thanksgiving Mass will be celebrated at the Blessed Sacrament Church, 14072 S. Olive, Westminster, at 6:45 p.m. Saturday, January 30, 1993 in honor of Rev. Dinh Ngoc Que.

Why is this Thanksgiving Mass so special?

According to a newsletter made known to local newspapers, the Mass is for Rev. Dinh Ngoc Que, a Redemptorist, a former chaplain for Phuoc Tuy subzone, Vung Tau special zone and military zone of the Capital, to officially offer Thanks to God for having been reunited with his spiritual and blood-related family members after thirteen years of imprisonment, and for being able to continue his pastoral duties.

The event is organized by Rev. Mai Khai Hoan and Rev. Tran Quang Diem with the participation of other priests and those who had served in the special military zone of the Capital, and the former teachers of Tinh Thần and Truyền Tin high schools.

For more information, please contact:

· Rev. Dinh Ngoc Que, (714)-534-5681
· St. Joseph Pharmacy, (714)-839-9343
· Rev. Mai Khai Hoan, (714)-893-3059

The Thanksgiving Mass is organized by Rev. Tran Quang Diem and Rev. Mai Khai Hoan, spiritual family

314

members and by Mr. And Ms. Phan Lan Anh and Mr. Dinh Ngoc Thu.

By the grace of God,

Rev. Dinh Ngoc Que, a Redemptorist, a former chaplain for the military zone of the Capital has just come to the United States to reunite with his blood-related and spiritual families after 13 years of imprisonment and to continue his pastoral duties. Rev. Tran Quang Diem, a senior priest of our spiritual family and I, a young family member, we would like to invite our fellow priests and everyone who had served in the Special Military Zone of the Capital to the Thanksgiving Mass which will be celebrated at the Blessed Sacrament Church, 14072 S. Olive, Westminster at 6:45 p.m. Saturday, Jan. 30, 1993.

After the Mass, everybody is invited to a tea party in honor of Rev. Dinh Ngoc Que in the reception room near the meeting hall in the parish grounds.

Your presence will be a great honor for us.
Respectfully,
Rev. Vincent Tran Quan Diem
Rev. Mic. Mai Khai Hoan

During the Mass, I shared my ideas with the Community as follows:
Dear brothers and sisters:

Before April 30, 1975, I decided to stay with the Communists in order to share joys and sorrows with my compatriots, particularly with those I had served as a chief chaplain for the Special Military Zone of the Capital, a district chief of Saigon diocese military region and the principal and director of Tinh Than high school.

My decision was blessed by God.

But just one month after the fall of Saigon, I had to report for reeducation and was detained ever since. It might be good to me, I think, as I had a chance to live and labor with my friends. Life in prison was not easy, by all means. We almost starved to death, sometimes. God however had given us enough strength to live and support one another by sharing our sufferings. In a spirit of solidarity, we tried to help Buddhist monks and Protestant ministers perform religious and social activities for believers and other detainees as well. During 13-year-period of imprisonment, we had to move to various camps, eleven times altogether. Wherever we went, we never forgot to help our friends spiritually.

On Jan. 13, 1988, I was set free by a decree of the Department of the Interior. After being released, however, I was not allowed to live with my Congregation. I was denied the right to do pastoral duties such as celebrating Mass, preaching, performing the Holy Sacraments... I was forced to live in hiding and work in secret for four or five years before I got the idea to leave the country for freedom.

The purpose of my departure is twofold:
First, to be able to do my pastoral duties in a free society, and second, to have an opportunity to see relatives, friends and other refugees and remind them of their homeland.

" Out of sight out of mind " is what I am afraid of. Therefore, I would like to remind my compatriots to learn from experience and try to unite in an effort to help our children achieve scholastically and succeed financially, so that they can return to Vietnam some day, as intellectuals, technicians, scientists to build a happy society and a prosperous country entirely free from authoritarianism.

It is my dream, and I think it's everybody's as well. So, I celebrate Mass today not only for me to thank God, but also to pray for a solid cooperation of all of us for the realization of our common dream. May God help our young generation become aware of their noble mission to secure a better future for themselves and also for their beloved homeland.

May God, the King of an endless spring, strengthen everybody's faith in the New Year.

After the mass, everybody crowded into the reception room. It was a really joyful and happy meeting. A few days later, I had an open letter of thanks printed on the Nguoi Viet daily news as follows:

First of all, I respectfully offer my heart-felt thanks to "God and St Mary for having bestowed upon me so many blessings, lovingly protected and carried me safely through all the difficult times and finally brought me to the United States.

I am deeply moved to think that God and Mary have called so many compassionate and generous people to welcome me and help me in a special way during my first days of resettlement in a foreign land.

Especially during the solemn Thanksgiving Mass organized in my honor at the Blessed Sacrament Church, Westminster, while standing before the prayerful attendance of my relatives, friends and the Community, I feel more clearly a special love God and Mary have for me.

I sincerely extend my thanks to Mgr Nguyen Duc Tien, director of the Vietnamese Catholics in the diocese of Orange County, to my spiritual uncle, Rev. Tran Quang Diem and my spiritual young brother, Rev. Mai Khai Hoan, associate pastor of Westminster parish, who have organized the Thanksgiving Mass for me.

I also would like to express my thanks to Rev. Chau Xuan Bau, vice provincial of the Redemptorist Congregation overseas, and my fellow priests, relatives, friends and the Community... My special thanks to members of various committees in charge of reception, safety and order, decoration, worship service, sacred music, food and drink... to members of the parish executive committee, to various groups, the association of catholic mothers, Hien Linh choir of Westminster parish... to all who have positively

contributed their efforts and energies to the full realization of this memorable event

Finally, I say thanks to my Godchildren Phan
Lan Anh at Saint Joseph Pharmacy and Lily's Bak-
ery' owners, my younger brother Dinh Ngoc Thu and
all members of the Dinh family.

May God, through Mary's intercession, bestow
his blessings upon monsignor, my fellow priests, relatives and friends, brothers and sisters.

I don't forget to send my special thanks to the
president, two directors and all members of the executive committee of Nguoi Viet Daily News.

Grateful Yours,

Dinh Ngoc Que

The Marian Day in Missouri

During my first year (1993) in the United States
the Congregation of the Mother Co-redemptrix invited me to attend the Marian Day at Carthage, Mis-
souri and to deliver a sermon during the Mass.

Before a large Catholic Community (about 40,000)
including those who came from as far as Canada,
France and Australia, I took the opportunity to promote the devotion of St Mary, and 117 Vietnamese
martyrs, reminding everybody to pray for Vietnam,
their homeland.

Following is the textual copy of my sermon:

" You are the honor of our nation" (Judith, 15g)
Queen of Vietnamese martyrs, pray for us!

Dear Brothers an Sisters,

The story I am going to tell you is what you cannot imagine. Do you know when the Holy See declared to canonize 117 Vietnamese martyrs, everyone in Vietnam rejoiced, especially the Catholics and people of good will. Yet the Communist government and those who followed them tried to raise suspicion and cause trouble. They flexed all their political muscles to kick off a campaign, trying to abort the Holy See's plan. They recruited so-called patriotic Catholics for their cause and called for the cooperation of a number of "state-owned " priests. They succeeded in winning some easy-going bishops' statements in their favor. They had the martyrs' private lives picked to pieces and reserved the right to review them under the light of their own political, secular and atheist point of view. It was so funny when they claimed victory and declared themselves entitled to select the martyrs, excluding from the list those who, they thought, should not be canonized. Seminars were organized on a large scale throughout the country from villages, districts to cities on the theme of canonization, especially on the list of 117 names that had been made public. The hottest topic at that time was the Vietnamese martyrs. It became headline-news on TV, Radio, and newspapers... All the Mass media, printed materials, photocopies were used to present the Vietnamese martyrs under the light of the government's view. The campaign went on day and night for several months.

Therefore, the whole nation, I might say, came to know about the canonization of Vietnamese martyrs, for some, to learn how Catholicism had come to Vietnam, for others, to know more details on the heroic lives of Catholic people who had accepted death in testimony of their faith. So much time and money were spent on the campaign. Yet, as you know, all their hard work and energy came to nothing.

Actually, the atheist communists had worked for free for the martyrs. On June 19, 1988, albeit the absence of the representatives of VN government, the council of Vietnamese bishops and the Catholics from Vietnam, the Holy See solemnly canonized 117 Vietnamese martyrs as planned. The event was a glory for Vietnam before the world, and particularly for the Vietnamese Catholic Community. It truly highlighted the splendid example of those heroes who had remained faithful to God till the end of their lives.

What did happen is ironically quite a reverse of what the Communists had expected. Is this a miracle? Yes, when witnessing the event at home, I had to admit that it was a miracle performed by the martyrs, intending to make themselves known as our heroic ancestors to all of us in the country including the non-Catholics. It was also a way of spreading faith and teaching religious doctrine.

Now, let us ask ourselves what force has made the martyrs brave enough to die for their faith. The answer is: Beside the supernatural strength given by the Holy Spirit, the martyrs are braced by another force. It is the one deriving from their devotion of St. Mary that I would like to stress on this Marian Day. "St. Mary, Mother of God, pray for us, sinners now and in the hour of death." They prayed with confidence to their Holy Mother during trying times, especially in the hour of death to keep their faith.

Testimonials are plentiful. Following are some of them:

In 1955, St. Andrew Nguyen Kim Thong, an elder in Go Thi parish council, had a special devotion of St. Mary. During the period of religious persecution, he was captured and sent to prison in the South. He had recited all seven Psalms and kept praying to St. Mary until he collapsed to death from exhaustion in his cell.

In 1962, Van Than group members stood impassively watching 200 men, 106 women and 50 children being burned alive in the grounds of Ba Ria church in the city of Phuoc Tuy. All those Catholics were killed while devoutly saying the rosary.

In 1863, St. Phillip Minh had bequeathed his Rosary to Mr. Minh, a chief of his village before being beheaded. He prayed in a loud voice: "Oh, St Mary, pray for me during this hour of death."

St. Le Bao Tinh said the Rosary, everyday and fasted on every Marian feast's eve. He used to say: "Two things come first. One is to love God, the other is to love Mary. To me, loving Mary is sufficient for our salvation, because she is the only way leading to God."

The above-mentioned stories are just among many proving the source of strength for the Vietnamese martyrs. No wonder we have a special devotion of Mary as we are the offsprings of those who were well-known for their love of Mary.

Before deciding to canonize 117 Vietnamese Martyrs, Pope John Paul II mentioned the faith-life and devotion of St. Mary of the Vietnamese. He said to a delegation of priests during an audience in Late October, 1987: "The Vietnamese family in Vietnam and abroad should become a school of prayer and faith, a character training institute and a center of apostolic activities. I earnestly entrust you and your nation to St. Mary's care. She is your real mother whom every Vietnamese Catholic venerates. May she keep you always in hope and courage..."

By those words, the Holy Father wanted us to keep the Vietnamese martyrs' spirit alive: to sacrifice everything, even our own lives for God and for our faith, to stick to St. Mary in joys as well as in sorrows. Now, as the martyrs' children, we have to follow in their foot-steeps: to come to God and Mary for help in any circumstance and to keep our faith to the end.

God is above everything. Mary is the queen, the honor of our nation.

I am thinking of the old woman who fled the

country in 1954, leaving behind everything, except the picture of the Mother of Perpetual Help, of so many people who since 1975 have risked their lives in a small, shaky boat in search of freedom. They have braved the stormy waves threatening to swallow them up on the way to freedom. In the most desperate situation, they did not give up hope, but kept saying the rosary, asking Mary for help, and miraculously, they made it safely to freedom. I am thinking of the former prisoners whose only solid rock to bank on is Mary and the Rosary; of various Communities in Vietnam as well as in the United States, who recite the Rosary everyday, perform flower offering ceremony and organize solemn processions in Mary's honor without being afraid of the atheist Communists or being affected by the material world. Generally speaking, the Vietnamese Catholics always keep their tradition of serving God and St. Mary.

Now, I would like to bring the matter closer to home. The concrete testimony is not to be found somewhere else. It is right here at Carthage where the Congregation of the Mother Co-redemptrix hosts the Marian Day annually, providing a chance for us, Mary's children from all over the world to congregate to proclaim our faith, to praise God and Mary and thank them for all the blessings we and our families have received. Together, let's pray to Mary, our mother for our homeland still plagued with many problems concerning economy, culture, society and religion.

We have to acknowledge that Mary is "the honor of our nation" and of every one of us, children of the martyrs. May the Queen of the Vietnamese martyrs pray for us, especially for our beloved homeland.

Glory to you, Mary!

Glory to you, Mary!

Glory to you, Mary!

Spring of Reunion

"Spring of Reunion" Festival organized by O.C. former political prisoners of South Vietnam is a special occasion for me to meet non-Catholic friends. The Nguoi Viet Daily News reported the event as follows:

Spring of Reunion Festival of Vietnamese political prisoners in Orange County.

Huntington Beach: A Spring of Reunion Festival hosted by the mutual assistance Association of O.C former political prisoners took place at Golden West College, Huntington Beach, last Sunday with the participation of about 2000 political prisoners, their families and guests. Present among them was Rev. Dinh Ngoc Que, a former Catholic officer in the Army of the Republic of Vietnam, a former Chief chaplain of Saigon military zone who had won the respect of many.

Editor's note: Rev. Dinh Ngoc Que has just left Vietnam for the U.S. to reunite with his family and the Catholic community of Southern California. On

the occasion of the "Spring of Reunion" Festival organized by former political prisoners of South Vietnam in Orange County, he did not hesitate to speak
out from a heart full of zeal and sincerity.

We would like to have his friendly talk printed
as a piece of advice and also as a norm of living for
himself and others in the U.S. (Titles and sub-titles
are given by the editor)

What do former political prisoners and their families have to do now?

Let's give a big hand to the Reunion Day and to
greet one another in the New Year day.

I just left Vietnam for the U.S. three weeks ago.
I feel so encouraged and moved to be present here,
today, the jubilant day of reunion, because after 13
years in the Communist concentration-camps in the
North, I find myself lucky to be alive and meet you
here, my friends, with whom I have terribly suffered
in mind and body for the sake of our homeland.

First of all, I would like to extend my thanks to
three following associations:

· The mutual assistance association of former
Vietnamese political prisoners.

· H.O association for the assistance of the war
disabled soldiers, orphans and widows.

· The Committee for the assistance of political
prisoners. You have the initiative and know how to
combine your effort in organizing this great reunion
day. As victims of a past society plagued with dis-

unity, division and self-proclaimed leaders who did more of the talking than doing, we have lost everything and ended up in prison. It is truly a bitter experience for all of us.

Let's continue to sacrifice
for the generation to come

By the grace of God, we survive. And now thanks to generous individuals and charitable organizations, we are able to come here and live in a free land.

Dear brothers and sisters, we readily accept to rebuild our lives in a foreign country just for the sake of our children and for the future of our country. The new situation might require more of our effort as more adversities might arise ahead. Armed with a prison wrought-iron will and with a source of strength coming from above, we can live a stronger life and stand firm as a good example for our children to follow and for the benefit of our beloved country. Let's not be tempted by an easy life of pleasure and enjoyment. Let's reject the idea of making up for the deprivations we have suffered. Haunted by bitter experiences of loss and suffering, we still maintain a complex of inferiority, adopt a negative attitude and want to live in selfish isolation. This is, however, a golden opportunity for us to turn sacrifice and suffering into something that can benefit our children. As an old generation, our responsibility is to support and help the young generation to make progress and succeed in life.

Honor and Success are for Vietnam

I also would like to take this opportunity to say a few words to young people living in 40 different countries in the world, particularly those living in the United States. Dear young friends, you are the young buds of the country, entitled to inherit the legacy of your predecessors. It's good luck; It's a blessing, I might say, for you while enjoying much comfort and freedom in a civilized world. Hold your head high, as you are of Vietnamese descent. On TV, radio and newspapers, everywhere, at home as well as abroad, you are being praised and applauded on academic achievements and on a great deal of initiative and endurance. Having a chance to contact many people who have come here before me, I am truly delighted to find that they have tried to go back to school, get a high degree and have a good job. Their children follow in parents' footsteps, trying hard to pursue academic studies or to make a living if the situation does not permit them to go back to school. In quite a few families, all the children are college-graduates, getting a satisfying job. As a generation on the rise, you are guaranteed a bright future. You should be proud of yourselves in front of others in the United States. You can go ahead and raise your voice as your voice is of great value and should be heard in American society.

Dear young friends, I often tell your parents and those belonging to the old generation that they have settled down now, but they must not forget that they have suffered a lot. They have paid a high price for freedom to come here not just for them, but also for their children and grandchildren, and for their homeland in need of their sacrifice and effort. That's what I've said to your parents. But my dream about you is more than that. I dream that after having succeeded in education and business, you must work in return for this country to which you owe your success. You should also remember Vietnam, your homeland, your ancestors' birthplace, still suffering from poverty, starvation and lack of modern technologies. I dream that you should bear in mind the difficult times and hardships your parents have undergone, and try hard to achieve academically and succeed financially, so that you may go home (or at least go back and forth) and together with your peers at home to build a Vietnam free of authoritarianism and monopoly. Vietnam in the future must be a rich and powerful country where every of its citizen can truly enjoy peace and happiness, a country worthy of its heroic forefathers' indomitable spirit.

On the New Year Day, I sincerely wish brothers and sisters, young friends and everybody a successful, peaceful and happy New Year. May God bless and protect us all.

Rev. Dinh Ngoc Que
Chief chaplain of Saigon Capital Military Zone,
District chief of Saigon Diocese Military region,
Principal and director of Tinh Than high school.

I am so grateful that coming to the United States, I can enjoy freedom and practice my pastoral duties as a priest. My wish for myself as well as for every Vietnamese living abroad is simply this:

· To bravely accept reality in order to fit in the new environment.

· To bravely accept reality in order to achieve something useful to a future Vietnam, our homeland.

Through St. Mary's intercession, the queen of Vietnam and the advocacy of the Vietnamese Martyrs who are our ancestors, God will bring Vietnam back to life. Everything of me comes from God's Grace: my past, my present and my future.

February 5, 1998
Dinh Ngoc Que

The English version
was completed on Memorial Day,
May 31, 1999 by
Tran Van Dien

Table of Contents

Lay-out & design: Dinh Phung Tien